Understanding Spirits

Paul Gater

www.capallbann.co.uk

Understanding Flower Spirits

Cover photograph by Mark Borg
Cover design by Paul Mason

Published by:

Capall Bann Publishing
Auton Farm
Milverton
Somerset
TA4 1NE

Contents

Introduction

'...the spring arose on the garden fair
Like the spirit of love felt everywhere...'
Percy Bysshe Shelley

A world without flowers – being denied the joy of their brightness of colour, scent and form – would be unthinkable. But exactly why should this be? We acknowledge their beauty yet we take flowers almost for granted. We feel so much the stronger when positively connected with other people, animals and especially our natural surroundings, including gardens, and particularly flowers. They are living presences, bringing harmony and meaning into our lives, far beyond anything we can create ourselves.

Some flowers were once regarded as gods in earthly form, being worshipped by peoples of many religious disciplines throughout the world, who attributed to them all sorts of magical potential. Floral motifs decorate our places of worship, heraldry, paintings, wallpaper, pottery ware, furniture, fabrics, items of jewellery, much of the bric-a-brac we see in souvenir shops. The power of that same spirituality in flowers has pervaded every part of our lives – even the language we use to communicate with each other. For example, we speak of someone being 'in the bloom of youth'; an older person with a 'late-flowering talent'; when we are optimistic we are viewing life 'through rose-tinted glasses'; someone now deceased is 'pushing up the daisies', and if things are really going well 'everything's coming up roses'.

My horticultural career has spanned over forty years and I have always regarded it as an intriguing and rewarding journey through all the different kinds of gardens I have encountered. With some I was involved in their maintenance, others I created or helped to create, and was fortunate to see a number of them become wholly established. For me it has been a case of trees, shrubs – and especially flowers – all the way and, increasingly over time, I have become more and more aware of their spirituality.

Conversely, during the journey, I also discovered that many of the people I met didn't appreciate flowers for what they really represent. I still encounter those who will go to great lengths – and expense – to get particular flowering plants for their gardens, not knowing the reason why, other than perhaps having seen them recommended by some television guru. Today's status symbols, perhaps? By contrast, our ancestors looked upon flowers as a source of power and magic, as important a part of their lives as their awareness of nature's varied seasonal rhythms of wonder and colour.

The current proliferation of books, magazines and television programmes about all aspects of horticulture from hard landscaping, planting trees and shrubs, to cultivating vegetables and flowers, has made us all aware of the wonderful opportunities open to us. Not only can we 'do our bit' to help improve the environment, but we can also appreciate the sense of being guided along the garden path towards that same spirituality, incredible power and magic of flowers, as experienced by our ancestors long ago.

It is said that when Gautama Buddha (Prince Siddharta, prior to his attaining an existence of meditation and asceticism) was asked to define Enlightenment, he simply smiled, and held up a flower in one hand, turning it between his fingers. His silent answer symbolised a transcendence that lay beyond definition by mere words.

The immensely uplifting feeling of seeing, experiencing and being near to flowers, especially if we have grown them ourselves, can make us very aware of their deeper significance. What can be better to revive the spirit than to sit in the garden after a long day's work (even if only for half-an-hour), revelling in the exquisite shades and colours? It doesn't have to be a large area, a few potted plants may be just as potent - even a single bowl of strongly-scented hyacinths on the window-ledge indoors can have the same effect. Our household derives an enormous amount of pleasure from a bowl containing several cacti that surprise us by flowering intermittently over the year.

Presenting or being presented with a flowering plant or a bunch of cut flowers is a wonderful token of apprec-iation, celebration or communication, offered in the true spirit of the blooms themselves. The flowers' continuing iridescence of being has always punctuated our lives, not only spiritually but practically too, even being used as sources of healing for our injuries and ailments.

As this book is concerned with investigating flower spirits, the types and varieties of flowering plants are obviously referred to, although I have not gone into detail about their raising and subsequent cultivation. I did not feel it was necessary, as there are so many excellent books easily available on the subject. I have referred to most plants and flowers by their common, more well-known, names. Latin names have been kept to a minimum – used only where the relevant subjects are not known by any other.

A big thank-you to the following people for talking to me, contributing their thoughts and comments which have added so much to this book:

Tehsin Ahmid, Martin Colclough, Alice Crick, Diana Smith, Marion Boon, Pauline Hart and Ian Rattray. Thanks also to my wife Dilys Gater, without whom this book might not have been written!

I have included short interviews which I feel open up the wider perspectives of the subjects discussed at the end of each chapter. These are given in the words of the interviewee.

Flowers are steeped in their own traditional lore and power, so gentle yet so completely pervasive that claims have been made that their iridescence marks the presence of the flower faeries themselves – whatever name they are given or whatever form they take. Obviously, because there is a huge body of English tradition and folklore regarding flowers, I have drawn on this quite heavily. But this book is not just confined to the British Isles. As you will see, the flowers and their traditions originate from all over the world.

One thing is certain. It is the very purity of flowers – from no matter where – that welcomes us into the world, continuing to sustain us throughout our own seasons of growth and aspiration, nurturing peace and intuition within us even if only for a few moments at a time. Flowers put us in touch with our own deepest spirituality, though we are not always aware. They accompany us, marking our rites of passage. Their beauty – some only achieving a brief flowering of hours rather than days – signifies our desire to reach our own finest potential. And it is the coming together of spiritualities – theirs and our own – that gently ease our passage when the time comes for us to take leave of this 'mortal coil'.

Paul Gater

Chapter One

Looking for the Spirits

A primrose by a river's brim
A yellow primrose was to him
And it was nothing more.

William Wordsworth

Remember those days of childhood magic when, as human beings, we were still intuitively in touch with nature, aware of the positive energies of flowers? Glorious days when we sat on some sunny lawn, making 'daisy-chains'; running off into the woods in late spring and returning with armfuls of wilting bluebells (now forbidden, of course), pulling a petal off a buttercup flower, and holding it to the throat - if it reflected on the skin, we were supposed to like butter. Oh, the thrill of carefully opening a snapdragon with thumb and forefinger, not knowing what might be inside – a gossamer unit of energy, a faery, perhaps?

Today's children still reach up to touch the leaves and blossom of a tree, or pull off a flower from someone's wisteria on their way to school. We are all of us at the many different stages on that journey through life, like parts of some great simultaneous equation.

We can relate too to other extra dimensional experiences – sometimes many of them - that we may have had as children. I certainly recall a small 'invisible friend' called Tom, having intriguing conversations with him in my bedroom! I never told my parents about him, not because I might have been laughed at, but simply because he was my secret – my secret companion into the magical realms. I like to think it was Tom who was the first to awaken my spiritual awareness to those deeper kingdoms of Nature – the animals, birds, the overwhelming feeling of other dimensions experienced in the physical freedom of the fields and bluebell woods that surrounded our village in those days. Whether or not Tom was a genuine little 'spirit friend', or a wiser extension of myself, I can't quite decide. But I'm very grateful to him.

As we grow up we lose that initial magic of childhood – if it was magic – an initiation into another life that lay just beyond the back door of home. I'm not so sure we lose all of it, because some of us retain that ability, that sixth sense, to access those other 'wavelengths'. Some think that as we grow and more mundane concerns come crowding in, our interests expand in the here and now and 'spirit friends' get thrown out with the toys and childhood. But as we mature (or perhaps learn wisdom) we long to enter once again through that glorious gateway to those other dimensions. This may come when least expected – following some family, health or financial crisis, even just by witnessing a natural revelation like an exceptional sunrise or sunset. How magical is the translucence of red or pink camellia flowers emblazoned against the fading light of dusk.

Historically, these things were recognised in all cultures: the natural world was endowed by a realm of creative intelligence in the form of nature spirits. Many people still believe it is these spirits who are responsible for the natural laws that maintain everything in proportional balance regarding our planet, the Earth. As such, flowers were even looked upon as divine presences in the past. Nothing to do with 'childish imagination', this was a deep spiritual truth.

This is so even today – something that might surprise a lot of people. Mark, a tough, former soldier, told me that when he discovered vandals had been in his garden, he was so distraught he apologised to his African marigolds after their flowers had been broken off. But we must not be misled by appearances. The fragile beauty of flowers can be deceptive – therein lie powerful forces which, at the same time, also give out an equilibrium of love and light. Parallel to a flower's outer beauty, there is an invisible one – what the Q'uero people (directly descended, it is believed, from the old Inca priests) of the southern central Peruvian mountains call the 'yoque', as opposed to the mundane, everyday life referred to as 'panya'.

We all know those who live by 'panya' alone – their lives are bound up by petty detail and hair-splitting dogma, too much attention paid to the small and the unimportant. I met Nora when she was employed as a cleaner for an elderly couple who had a large garden I knew well, since I had maintained it for some years. One of the features I regarded as most striking was a beautiful self-sown cotoneaster that cascaded out from between two tall conifers in a corner. Its mass of small white flowers on long, arching branches in midsummer were followed every autumn by a myriad red berries.

"That thing needs ripping out!" said Nora, one day. "After all, it is only a weed!"

A few months before, she had cast similar judgement on a magnificent Clematis Montana growing on a nearby wall, complaining that, after flowering, the fallen petals would have to be swept up then, later, all the leaves. She was more aware of the fine plant as a potential source of 'untidiness' than breathtaking beauty.

Sometimes, as I've discovered, it's best to say nothing. That way you – and the flowering plant – finish up by surviving!

How sad that there are so many people who seem bent on imposing their own lead-lined view of the world, always eager to criticise and find fault, while at the same time being totally unmoved by any desire to capture even a glimpse of those 'fathomless heights' available to us all.

During the many years I have been self-employed, I regularly maintained a number of gardens and got to know them well. I found it fascinating how they reflected the personalities and spiritual awareness – or lack of it – of the people who owned them.

Myra was a middle-aged 'lady who lunched' with a company director husband. One day she told me rather haughtily that she wanted the border I had just cleared and dug over to be planted with a riot of summer colour, together with other colour interest for as long a season as possible. A showy display to impress her friends was what she had in mind.

I began by planting several shrubs informally for flowers/ foliage and winter-coloured bark effects at the back. Some herbaceous plants were grouped likewise further forward, for a succession of more subtle summer colour. I kept the really bright subjects – mainly annuals – planted more to the front. The effect was finely balanced, but when the border was approaching its best, Myra did a U-turn and told me she thought there was "Too much colour!"

Twelve months later, when we were both standing by the same border which was displaying an even more garish splurge of vulgarity, she declared approvingly that this was much more sensible! Well, there's no pleasing some people. I had thought all the flowers very spiritual. But alas, they were not so through Myra's eyes. She only saw what she wanted to see.

Ruby, a widow and retired cabaret artiste in her late seventies, was one of my more treasured clients. Little had been done to her garden for some time before I arrived to lick it into shape, yet the place abounded in happiness, good health - and masses and masses of flowers. Clematis, honeysuckle, roses, lavender, troughs of pansies were in full glory, despite the brambles and hummocks of long grass growing here and there.

It was over coffee and biscuits one morning during my 'break' that Ruby secretly admitted to me how she talked to her flowers every day. "They're my manna from Heaven, dearie!" she said – which just about summed it up.

'A weed is but an unloved flower.'
                                        Ella Wheeler Wilcox

Alan, in his late forties, was the high-flying owner of a northern business school. I encountered him at a Summer Fair at Hartington, in the Peak District where we chatted about the cottage gardens in the village. He said that, although he liked flowers, he rarely had time to bother with them in his own garden – in fact, he said, he thought there was nothing spiritual about them at all. But later in the conversation, when we had moved on to the subject of 'ghosts' (one of my books is titled *Living With Ghosts*), he mentioned how as a small child he too had had a special 'invisible friend', 'a little lad in old-fashioned silk pyjamas', whom he used to play with on the stairs.

Because she couldn't see who he was talking to, his mother worried he might be going mad. His father, a quiet man who was sometimes the butt of jokes among their neighbours, said nothing at first. But one day, this keen gardener revealed a secret to his son: every summer, he saw flower faeries in the garden, down on the herbaceous border.

"At last I knew why the neighbours laughed at him, but I believed him," Alan said, adding significantly, "even though, in this case, it was me who saw nothing!"

Here was a man who had never considered himself spiritual? I thought otherwise although Alan would probably have dismissed such beliefs as 'kids' stuff'. Well, maybe - but they are part of our early education, our initiation into the true secrets of living. In time, he too may be able to own his true feelings without embarrassment or a sense he is somehow not being macho or tough enough. The regard he has for his garden may transform him into the better, more enlightened individual he could become, realising every tree or flower has its own personality, power and spiritual dimension, its own 'song' to sing, whether an award-winning rose at the Flower Show or a clump of rosebay willow-herb growing on some obscure railway embankment.

So many people, I think, fail to simply accept flowers for what they are. And by having their personal likes and dislikes, even over the way the flowers are planted – formally or informally – they miss out on such a lot, as a result being totally unaware of flower spirituality.

Something Sacred

Though we feel that giving a beautiful bouquet is something special, it is surprising how many people still regard a flower as just an object, attractively shaped, with pretty colours, and scent thrown in for good measure. Scientifically, plant physiology is not yet fully understood but a flower does represent part of a plant's (including cacti, grasses, trees) reproductive process. Via colour or scent (or both), insects are attracted for purposes of pollination. Some plants are more dependent on the wind for the same process to occur. But every flowering plant – no matter which genus – possesses its own field of energy, something sacred to itself that cannot be explained by matter-of-fact scientific reasoning. Many botanists themselves recognise this. And as John Ruskin (1819-1900) succinctly put it:

'We cannot fathom the mystery of a single flower, nor is it intended that we should; but that the pursuit of science should constantly be betrayed by the love of beauty, and the accuracy of knowledge by tenderness of emotion.'

Perhaps the ancients would have agreed, having always been aware of Nature as a world of spirit and energy. It was widely acknowledged that plants passed on their healing abilities to those individuals who were able to 'tune in' to their spiritual wavelength and, in turn, communicated back to the plants. Such individuals were known as shamans, or wise ones, who often lived by themselves in huts or caves. Many still practise in the world today, in indigenous cultures like the Australian Aborigines, North and South American Indians, the tribes of Africa, and the peoples of Indonesia, Tibet and Siberia – without ever coming into direct contact with each other. It is interesting to speculate whether they would all have evolved such techniques independently, or whether they represent the last vestiges of a knowledge that once existed world-wide.

The latter is perhaps more likely. So-called 'primitive tribes' are far more sophisticated spiritually than civilised man. During certain religious ceremonies – sometimes lasting for days – they are able to heighten even more their states of consciousness by means of dancing, drumming, chanting *en masse* and ingesting hallucinatory drugs.

In his brilliant essay *The Doors of Perception* (1954), the writer Aldous Huxley describes how he first took mescalin, an hallucinatory drug extracted from the sacred peyote cactus of Mexico. Huxley was unusual in that, literary giant though he happened to be, he was also intensely interested in science, particularly regarding the human mind. It was his belief that information the human mind did not need to remember any more in order for us to survive as a race – such as our ancient knowledge of the natural order of things and our own affinity with it – somehow got sifted out. We might now think of ourselves as being totally equipped to tackle the rigours of today's fume-filled concrete maze of a world, but having sacrificed our 'sense of wonderment' as a result.

Intriguingly, as the mescalin took over, one of the first things Huxley saw as his normal visionary boundaries diminished was 'a bunch of flowers shining with their own inner light.'

Following on in the 'Swinging Sixties', a whole younger generation was seized by the desire to emulate those aspects of Eastern culture thought most likely to bring the individual closer to Nirvana. With San Franscisco as its 'epicentre', incorporating psychedelic drugs, the power of pop music, sexual freedom, the cult of the Flower Children, reconsidered half a century on, might be thought of as a general mix that lacked a certain focal commitment. Yet put into context with ominous Cold War developments at the time, perhaps it was infinitely more successful than we realise, despite the tragic casualties left lying in its wake. Maybe we still remember those images of Flower Power more vividly than those of the Cuban Missile Crisis of the same decade.

By gradual erosion, thanks to our own Western culture, we have been isolated, to varying degrees, from the natural world by life on the cutting edge, existing superficially, many people giving little thought to those other, very personal, dimensions awaiting exploration - dimensions of all sorts, of course.

Making contact with the natural spirits is what most of us are unconsciously doing when we take, say, a lunch-break stroll in the park. We enjoy sitting in the sun reading a book, or running about just for the fun of it – as we would on the beach. Once again, we are seized by an all-pervading sense of freedom, activating body and soul, just as in the days when we dashed through those fields and bluebell woods of childhood. Our energies will be revitalised by the spirits of nature at all times of our lives, if we will let them.

This is certainly true as we absorb the spirituality of a garden full of flowers, lingering perhaps over the thrill of an uninvited 'guest' – a wildflower or self-sown progeny of some choice perennial from a neighbouring garden. Add to this the effect of the dawn chorus, knowing the particular feathered individuals who visit the bird-table. In the changing rhythms at dusk we may witness the silent flit of the bats, and moths of various sizes drawn to those flowers that haven't closed down for the night.

A recent TV programme I found very positive and uplifting concerned a group of people enjoying life on their allotments in a Birmingham suburb. Amid the sunshine and burgeoning vegetables and flowers, the whole mood and atmosphere of the place was encapsulated by an elderly Jamaican-born lady. She exuded the sheer joy of living stemming from the things she grew and harvested, together with the wonderful camaraderie on tap from her fellow allotment-holders.

'Pure blood, and noble blood, in the fine and rose-fed veins;
Small, interspersed with jewels of white gold
Frail-filigreed among the rest;
Rose of the oldest races of princesses, Polynesian
Hibiscus.

Eve, in her happy moments,
Put hibiscus in her hair,
Before she humbled herself, and knocked her knees with repentance.'

D H Lawrence

A Partnership

We have become more aware of things spiritual in recent years, more appreciative of the need for sacred time and space, sometimes achieved independent of the recognised religions. Or is it, perhaps, a matter of actually embracing the Old Religion – that of our ancient ancestors? If so, this helps us to view life in a hugely different light. The exasperating car journey to and from work, the pressures of sitting at a computer all day in an airless office, the soulless monotony of working on a conveyor-belt system all take their toll. The habit of stifling mounting anger and frustration is something our bodies are not designed to endure.

In the natural way of things, by the rule of 'fight or flight', our ancestors would have turned to face the foe, or run off into the forest. Our 21st century situation doesn't allow us such privileges. Yet by adopting the old values, ideally we may be able to banish those subversive, negative feelings, even if it doesn't actually change the prevailing situation and the nearest natural thing many may see in the course of their working day will be a lone rubber-plant at the reception-desk, or the red carnation in the button-hole of the boss's jacket.

Attaining a balance between the physical and spiritual realms, we become so aware of the sacredness of everything that surrounds us. Spirituality, I feel, is very definitely a two-way thing, a partnership, as we've already perceived in the spirit world of the shaman. To receive from the flowers, we have to 'open up' and at the same time make available our spirituality for them – and, consequently, for our fellow-beings. So by thinking good about the flowers, we can all prosper.

Our ancestors venerated flowers to such an extent that they included them in acts of worship, adding their own especial spirituality to ritual and ceremony celebrating and invoking the deity or deities. The natural elements of Earth, Air, Fire and Water were believed to have their own sacred spirits, naiads, dryads and other earth entities – in some religions, these were even elevated to the ranks of gods or goddesses.

Sources of water – rivers, springs, streams and wells – all had their magical potential recognised, particularly in the east, while the Celts, Greeks and Romans offered gifts to the wells and waters – the Romans in the name of the goddess Fontanalia. The nymphs of streams and springs were also invoked.

In Britain today, old traditions link flowers and waters in the ancient ceremonies of Well Dressing. Some village wells are still regarded as sacred to the goddess Brighde, or Bride. When Christianity arrived on these shores, the Christian Church incorporated the worship of the pagan Bride with its own Saint Bridget and the colourful ceremonies continued. Now they are annual events that draw crowds.

In the village of Tissington, Derbyshire, for instance, the Well Dressing ceremony, together with a church blessing, takes place two weeks prior to Ascension Day and offers thanks for the inhabitants having survived a particularly severe period of drought during the early 1600s. Their own natural water supply had remained abundant throughout. Traditionally, the celebrations may be of even earlier origin, reaching as far back into the past as 1340, when the villagers escaped an outbreak of bubonic plague (the Black Death) that was then ravaging the population of Europe. They attributed their miraculous escape to the purity of their spring water – though more logically, the extreme isolation of the village could have been their salvation.

Well Dressing ceremonies involve 'dressing' or decorating the source of water, whether well, spring or tap, with boards onto which thousands of flower petals are attached to make up pictures, often from the Bible. This highly skilled process is an ancient art form still undertaken by the villagers themselves, sometimes carrying out a family tradition of many generations. Large boards are moistened, then placed face upwards on trestles so that they can be lined with clay. The design of the picture is 'traced out' with a sharp object and then the long process of 'petalling' can begin.

Apart from the petals, other plant materials such as bark, cones, grasses, large dried leaves or mosses are incorporated in the design, while the faces of characters portrayed are usually painted on clay. In some Welsh counties there is an Easter custom of scattering flower petals over the immediate vicinity of certain wells, and in other places the wells (known as 'clootie wells') are decorated with rags.

Communication with the spirits of nature reflects the sense of awe and wonder we feel when in the presence of things beyond ourselves, what our ancestors called 'the Mysteries'. Flowers have always been there when the Mysteries were celebrated or approached. Well Dressings are perhaps the most enduring ceremonies open to the public at large, but the prevalence of Flower Festivals, Flower Queens and the like help to keep alive that sense of participation, the colour, dignity and magic of flowers both representing, and speaking for, the divine.

A Place of Peace - Diana Smith

Diana is a textile artist, gardener and jam-maker. Her business is carried out under the name 'Jam Today'. These are her thoughts about the garden being a place of peace and tranquility, an essential antidote to life's traumas. They were written at a time when she was experiencing the demands of caring for an elderly, family relative.

'When my boundaries closed in on me, after my father's death, I knew that if I accepted the restrictions of caring for my mother it was essential that I found a way to make this into something positive and not a trap. If I permitted myself to resent those restrictions, it would make caring an impossibility, and would also destroy us both.

'As a gardener, when I need to release tension I turn compost, or dig a bed at the allotment. When I need to create order I tie in the raspberry canes or create a framework for the cordon fruit. When I need to nurture I prick out seedlings or gently divide perennials. When I need to observe – or look for inspiration – there is more in this small space than I can begin to understand, or express, in the rest of my lifetime.

'I have learned to perceive tiny differences of colour, trying to distinguish different varieties of my favourite hardy geraniums. I probably am unable to see a flower colour in isolation, because it is linked with its architecture, textures and energy. If I see a blue of the Siberian Iris, I will think of the way that it is rooted deep down in my bog garden. Also the way that its green leaves take on swirling new life in mid-spring, and the tall, thin spears it throws up as well as the amazing structure of the flowers and the great splash of blue in May.

'As an artist, my perceptions of what colour "means" comes from many different sources. I learned enough about colour theory, to have an awareness of how colours can affect each other – primary, secondary, complementary and tertiary.

'I am acutely aware of the changes that the seasons make to the colours around us. This is perhaps intensified by my enclosed world, or when I go to the allotment along the lane, or through the spinney to my mother's flat three or four times a day.

'My three cats, who also see the garden as their whole world with something of the same intensity, each have their own private places hidden away amongst the burgeoning plants. My daughter will take time to look at things I point out to her, and has her own relationship with parts of the garden. My husband sees it as my place and ventures into it no more than two or three times a year. When I bring occasional visitors round, I know they are seeing it only as a moment in time, and not as a continuous process of changing the garden from a barren place, of grass and tall, dark Leylandii hedging, to a space often on the verge of chaos, but teeming with life. For example, this year, the honeysuckles I planted some while back, have now made a dense thicket. As the cats sink into a sleepy, purring senility, the blackbirds have nested successfully.

'In the late evenings of midsummer, it is the blackbirds that take up certain vantage points, one favouring the cypress tree at the edge of my garden. One takes the Scots pine that overhangs the allotment, while another the aerial above my mother's flat.

'These three, positioned at the points of the triangle of my enclosed world, sing to one another.

'I am bound up in the ancient, simple, agrarian rhythms of day and night, seedtime and harvest. I learn to know the structures of the individual plants that crowd the spaces. I know those that will survive the ravages of winter and those that require cosseting to see a second summer. I discover where the various birds nest, and the lace wing moths hibernate. I spot the trees favoured as starling roosts by the dividing flocks in the winter evenings. At the spring equinox I wait for the purring of the emerging frogs, and by the solstice I am picking the first strawberries.

'And so it is that for most of the time I feel I have been given the gift of an enchanted world. A rare place of both stillness and energy, work and play.'

Chapter Two

A Walk to the Paradise Garden

'Soon will the high Midsummer pomps come on,
Soon will the musk carnations break and swell,
Soon we shall have gold-dusted snap dragon,
Sweet William with his homely cottage smell,
And stock in fragrant blow.'

Matthew Arnold

From the time of our earliest civilisations we have had the visualisation of life as a journey. We work towards some ideal and, common to many different religions, that ideal is a place of ultimate safety, upliftment and achievement – often perceived as a beautiful garden. Conversely, we might say that, once achieved, it simply represents journey's end. So wherever there is a beautiful garden, and the presence of flowers, they admit us to an ultimate of sorts – a point where we can reconnect, harmonise with their strength and magical powers.

These aspects of flowers have been used very much in heraldry. The lily, for example, is often depicted as a stylised fleur-de-lis (as well as the iris), or even simply as its natural self. The fraise plant, or white cinquefoil, is depicted as a strawberry flower and is used on the coat of arms of the Fraisers. The rose, amongst other things, has represented most famously the two powerful medieval Houses of

Lancaster and York, the families who fought each other in the War of the Roses (1455-85). The red rose symbolised Lancaster, the white rose stood for York. The red and white Tudor rose, discovered growing in Wiltshire, was later adopted to symbolise the union of these two Houses on the marriage of Henry Tudor to Elizabeth of York in 1485.

Countries, too, have adopted floral emblems, such as Japan (chrysanthemum), a symbol of prosperity and longevity, the 16-petalled flower being the crest of the emperor. The Paulownia, a native flowering plant of China became the heraldic emblem of the imperial family. Then there is Wales (daffodil), Scotland (thistle), Austria (edelweiss), South Africa (protea), Hungary (tulip), India (lotus), Indonesia (jasmine), South Korea (Rose of Sharon), Ukraine (sunflower). Even the most humble residential places may reflect the flowers - 'Mimosa Cottage', 'Syringa House', Forget-me-not Lane, Magnolia Road, Laburnum Way, Wisteria Drive, for example. Superficially, they may often seem 'tacky', but they do represent a compliment to the spirituality of flowers, nonetheless.

A source of rest and peace, a garden can also be a potent source of stimulation. Realisation of this was probably what prompted our hunting forefathers to 'stake out' their territories and settle in family and community groups, learning to work with nature rather than against it, as is still practised by many of our indigenous peoples today. They were also to develop an ongoing awareness of the deity, their response being to create gardens – not just for their beauty, but also for the more practical means of growing food and for their medicinal potential.

Bearing close similarity, myths about the first primordial man and woman abound almost universally. In the Biblical Old Testament, for example, information is presented using the code of the Cabbala in a potent mixture of speculation, logic, inspiration and mathematics, each story inevitably containing symbolic references. Early man's vision of Paradise on Earth predated the Bible by thousands of years. The word 'Paradise' didn't actually appear in the Bible until translated by the Greeks after 200 AD, the original word *'Pairi daezi'* being an ancient Persian word meaning a walled or enclosed garden.

Paraðise on Earth

'Man was lost and saved in a garden.'

Blaise Pascal

The Bible tells us that the first man and woman (Adam and Eve) were created in a perfect garden called Eden, meaning 'delight' – a place now lost in the mistiness of time, like the walled garden of Alcinous, described in Homer's *Odyssey*, not to mention the famous Hanging Gardens of Babylon. In Eden grew the tree of knowledge, bearing the fruit of good and evil. Because Adam succumbed to Eve's enticements, taking a bite of the fruit against the will of God, both he and Eve were banished from Eden in disgrace, indicating that Mankind was doomed. Believers in the Cabbala suggested it was only logical that Adam and Eve would seccumb to temptation. Yet it could be said that their action represented the first stage of Man's development, rather than his doom. Otherwise, with its beauty, repose and tranquillity, Eden could have encouraged little else but stagnancy of the human spirit. Man would have been denied his learning curve and, besides many other things, his respect for the spirituality of the whole of Nature and her flowers.

So, although many of us today see the journey of life as moving towards some sort of Nirvana or Paradise, our own personal garden of beauty, repose and tranquillity, it could be construed as a journey in reverse. On the other hand, considering that modern civilisation forces us to constantly redefine our meaning of Paradise, perhaps we are still intent on that route forward after all. Hence the magnificent gardens worldwide, built according to the ideals of the different peoples who constructed them. Gardens have continued to develop over several thousand years, alongside our own evolvement.

There exists a mural from approximately 1400 B.C., the earliest surviving document, showing an ancient Egyptian garden, although it is known that there were such walled gardens in existence as far back as 3000 B.C. Far from being fairly crude, the mural shows real sophistication, the garden depicted being symmetrically designed, with trees, lots of fruit, flowers, water, fish and birds. Vines would have been trained against all walls. Such gardens were usually connected to the temples, plants and flowers being grown for ritualistic purposes. Other gardens, or oases, would have been located in the cities or on the edge of the desert, offering shade and refreshment to the weary traveller as a brief, but welcome, respite from a hot climate.

The Greek philosopher and writer Theophrastus, also a great gardener, was the first systematic classifier of plants, (hundreds of years prior to the more famous Linnaeus), and in 300 B.C. he was also first to establish the world's first botanic garden.

It was after the Roman Invasion of Britain in 55 B.C. that horticultural activity became very important, not only because of the spiritual, or aesthetic, aspect, but also for more practical reasons. The rich Romano-British owned splendid villa gardens, bright with colourful flowers, enclosed by walls in town or by hedging if located in the countryside. Gardens were basically rectangular, sometimes with curves incorporated to make a perfect arc, a terrace linking house and garden with a pergola of climbing plants, vines and statuary. Less wealthy citizens had smaller gardens and grew their plants and flowers mainly in pots. Given a larger area of land, the owner of a country villa would grow certain root vegetables, salads, parsley and asparagus, besides fruit trees and, of course, a vineyard. In fact, prior to the Romans coming to Britain we had never experienced such intensive crop-growing activities. Now there were more mouths to feed, including those of an occupying army!

Once abandoned after the slow Roman withdrawal during the 4th century A.D., their gardens soon faded, as did many other aspects of their culture. But as Christianity became more firmly established, the monks and nuns celebrated the glory of God by creating miniature Gardens of Paradise here on Earth, in the form of monastic gardens. These were situated round the monastery, while a rectangular area of grass surrounded by the cloister was usually divided in four parts by an intersecting path, representing a sign of the cross, sometimes with a fountain or well at the central point – no flowers – for the monks to use as a place of spiritual contemplation. The herb garden, with its medicinal plants, was situated to the North, near to the hospital, or infirmary. On the East side – most significantly – where the Church looked towards sun rise and the Holy City of Jerusalem – was the flower garden, symbolically rich, and used as a source of blooms to decorate the High Altar.

Many of the plants held great religious significance. The Madonna Lily, for example, represented the purity of the Virgin Mary; so, too, the white rose. Lady's mantle and Lady's bedstraw also referred to the Mother of Christ, while two shrubs that represented the saints were St. Dabeoc's heath and St. John's wort. The latter was named after John the Baptist, not only because of the red pigment it produces, symbolic of the blood shed when he was beheaded, but because it also flowers on his feast day at Midsummer.

Images of gardens and their flowers adorn the writings and folklore of Europe, the Middle East and beyond, into Asia, all representing a form of Paradise of the soul, a hint of what is to come. The emperors of China and Vietnam actually had their tombs constructed in beautiful and tranquil gardens of flowers, which they would often visit – and where they would eventually be laid to rest.

The quest for Paradise on Earth still continues. Though many medieval gardens did not survive to the present day, some examples have been lovingly recreated from old plans on their original sites. Later, very large, resplendent gardens were built, the grandeur of those at Versailles, for example, representing the munificence and power of absolute monarchy – the Sun King – Louis XIV himself. Similar gardens were also constructed in this country, as well as all over Europe, for patrons to display their personal wealth and power, formal topiary, knot-gardens, mazes included, with conifers and other evergreen subjects employed as dot-plants.

The Victorian era abounded with the introduction of exotic plants from all over the world, probably with more of an eye on commercial demand rather than on their spiritual aspect. Many were grown, thanks to the new technology of the day, under glass. Others that were hardy enough soon became adjusted to the English climate. The adventures of the actual plant hunters who risked their lives in hostile territories – and in some cases, lost them – would make a fascinating book in itself. As towns spread into the countryside many more people had gardens to cultivate. These still tended to be formal, with regimented clipped flowering trees and shrubs, but gradually, through the advocacy of William Robinson, a writer of gardening books in the 1880s, styles began to lean more towards a more natural look.

In the late 19th and early 20th centuries, the famous creator Gertrude Jekyll who, in her younger days had trained as an artist, worked out many planting schemes to form different flower associations so that they had the utmost effect, beautifully blended colour-wise but looking extremely natural. Her influence on planting schemes and garden design is still felt today.

From a much earlier era, Sir Thomas Moore (1478–1535) has been credited with establishing possibly the first 'English' garden, devoid of the European extravagances of the day in its simplicity and sensibility of design, as portrayed in the background to a surviving painting of Moore and his family. In 1520 he purchased land by the Thames in Chelsea village and set up a farm, the farmhouse surrounded by a very fine garden of trees, fruit and flowers. Part of his envisaged Utopia realised, perhaps?

Paradise of the Spirit

In 637 A.D. the Arabs conquering Persia became responsible for the continuing evolution of the so-called Paradise garden, introducing more intricate geometric patterns in the name of Islam, particularly with regard to the supremely tiled courtyards. Such gardens are still to be seen in Spain and North Africa, today. According to Islam, gardens of perpetual bliss here on Earth are but a foretaste of what will be experienced in the afterlife. Besides praying to God (Allah) for admittance, Islam teaches us that we should ask for the highest place in Paradise, of which it is written:

'They will live among sylvan forests where there is neither thorn nor bramble, amidst wildly flowering trees that provide cool, expansive shade. There are flowing brooks and fruits of all kinds that never go out of season nor diminish. They will recline in places of honour, With specially created companions who are pure, Undefiled, loving and of a similar age.'

Qur'an 56: 27-38.

Meanwhile, we are but the keepers of such places here on Earth. No garden, according to Islam, is regarded as complete without water, fish, birds, bees or butterflies. This, to my mind, is the perfect garden regardless of any religion. Islamic belief is that water should be included as channels, representing Paradise divided by four rivers. So tiled, but shallow canals (because of the scarcity of water) were constructed to flow north, south, east and west, taking the eye, mind and the spirit away from the inner world of the garden into the greater world beyond.

Besides things like apples, oranges and peaches, there would also be nut trees planted and Morello cherries, symbolising the fruits of the soul – all mentioned in the Koran. And, of course, there would be roses, important for their fragrance. Indeed, it is said that the first rose was created from a drop of perspiration that fell from the brow of the prophet Mohammed.

During the 6th and 7th centuries A.D. the Arabs went on to conquer parts of Asia, North Africa and Spain. Their style of garden was taken with them. But in India the gardens around temples were already very similar in their layout – walled, extremely symmetrical in design – beauty amid plants, flowers and water. That of the Taj Mahal is a good example, although constructed much later.

As we know, traditions are continually evolving and beautiful gardens created as a paradise for the soul – not all of Islamic origin – have, over many hundreds of years, reached all corners of the modern world. I recently enjoyed reading a lovely and inspirational book *The Sanctuary Garden* by Christopher Forrest McDowell and Tricia Clark-McDowell. They have founded a 22 acre paradise, the world-renowned Cortesia Sanctuary and Center for Natural Gardening and Healing, near Eugene, Oregon, U.S.A.

The Garden Within

'For, lo, the winter is past
The rain is over and gone;
The flowers appear on the earth;
The time of the singing birds has come...'

The Song of Solomon

Thanks to the flowers – highly individual, like ourselves - it is possible for us all to make a new start in life at any time. This is because they emit a vibrant form of energy that if we are aware of it, inevitably has an uplifting effect upon that of our own. In fact, it has been shown by using a special photographic technique - Kirlian imagery, developed by Semyon Kirlian, a Russian medical technician, in the 1930s – that a field of energising force is produced by all living things, including inanimate objects such as rocks. Leaves and flowers produce unique patterns of force similar to those shown by iron filings in close proximity to a magnet, except that we able to see the imagery of the flower energies in incredibly beautiful colours.

Sight being one of our primary senses, we are able to use the different colours in the garden to consciously influence our emotions, to heighten our overall sense of well-being, to foster relaxation or even to stimulate. Too much red, for example, can be over-energising so should be toned down by adding pink, purple and white flowers. Too much blue, a relaxing colour, may on the other hand induce symptoms of indifference, inhibition and depression. Remember the Billie Holiday song *'I Got A Right To Sing The Blues!'*? By using colour therapy wisely, we are put in touch with the world of spirit as a whole.

All of this knowledge was familiar to the ancient Egyptians, who used the technique by which particular coloured gemstones – as opposed to flowers – were placed on specific areas of the body while the patient lay horizontally. Their different hues were directed down into the body with the help of sunlight. This was the basis of crystal healing which is still very much in use today, based on the energising properties of the variously coloured gemstones.

All flowers are capable of stimulating the 'feel good' factor, restoring balance and good health to specific areas of our own bodies. I have briefly mentioned the meridian system of energies, but another system, incorporating the seven chakras (yet another old word from the Sanskrit, meaning 'wheel') was first developed by the Indian yogis and is used by many alternative therapists today.

The system represents areas of an upward flowing energy from the base of the spine to the crown of the head and back again. In diagrams, the seven chakras are often shown as brightly-coloured flower-heads depicted in their relevant colours which concern, via their different aspects, our physical and psychological well-being. As with the meridians, if the energy flow becomes interrupted in any way, then a chain reaction may well set in, promoting negativity and illness, Each chakra possesses its own particular rate of energy vibrations unique to its own particular colour.

These are the seven main chakras:

1. Root Chakra

Base of the spine; concerned with spinal column, leg-bones, feet, large intestine. Colour – red. Warm, vigorous, masculine; connected to the earth. Very life affirming, it is also connected to bloodshed. Remember the red poppies of Flanders Fields? But this colour also stands for rebirth, and is symbolic of happiness in marriage. Connecting flowers – red geranium, hawthorn, poppy, salvia.

2. Sacral Chakra

Situated below the navel, promoting harmony and well-being in the lower abdomen, including digestive system and reproductive organs. Colour – orange. Like red, a positive energiser where appropriate, representing radiance and vitality. Can help to overcome persistent personal fears, even those 'hangovers' from childhood. Connecting flowers – lily, marigold, montbretia, nasturtium.

3. Solar Plexus Chakra

Above the navel, behind the stomach. Gives the feeling of being in control of a situation. Responsible also for solar plexus, liver, gall bladder, pancreas, spleen and stomach. Colour – yellow. Warm, stimulating, strongly symbolic of spring, promoting a very positive feeling, clear thought and reasoning. Representing too, in the Far East, holiness and the Afterlife. Connecting flowers – daffodil, forsythia, marigold, primrose, winter jasmine.

4. Heart Chakra

Located at centre of the chest. Responsible for blood circulation, heart and lungs, thymus gland and the immune system. Colours – green and pink. Gives feeling of goodwill to all. Connections with love, compassion. Green is the chief colour of nature and the most balanced. Freshness of spirit. Excellent for emotional problems, and protection from heart problems. Connecting flowers – hellebore, nicotiana, carnation, hawthorn, pink, passionflower, rose.

5. Throat Chakra

In the throat, immediately above the collarbone. Promotes trust, creativity and communication. Responsible for thyroid, lymphatic system. Colour – light blue. If someone's favourite colour, it is calming, restful. They will be generally stable and satisfied with their achievements. This colour can also stimulate thirst for knowledge and is physically beneficial to asthma and stomach ulcers. Connecting flowers – lobelia, pansy, rose.

6. Forehead Chakra (Third Eye)
Positioned in the centre of the forehead, slightly above the eyebrows. Area for perception, reasoning, clairvoyance. Also covers pituitary gland, central nervous system, left side of the brain. Colour – violet/purple. Colour of love, mysterious links with the unconscious. Connecting flowers – hyacinth, lobelia, pansy, iris, viola.

7. Crown Chakra
Found at the crown of the head, it has bearing on the pineal gland and right side of the brain. Colour – white. Considered to be the seat of consciousness, intuition, and gateway to the realms of spirit. Connecting flowers – crocus, geranium, iris, summer jasmine, lilac, rose.

The above mentioned flowers, of course, represent only a small proportion of those available, which is one of the reasons why we tend to feel uplifted and positive in a flower garden, abounding in so many colours. Those relevant to our personal needs, even though we may not be conscious of the fact, are working on our chakras, invigorating us and realigning our energy flow, restoring it to what it should be. The energies assist us to feel positive and 'alive'– eliminating negative thoughts about returning to work after the holidays, or dealing with bills demanding our attention. Or, more profoundly, even helping us to face life again following an illness or some emotional crisis.

'And I will make thee beds of roses
And a thousand fragrant posies.'

Christopher Marlow

Flower essences can have a very great affect on us on a much deeper emotional level, akin to spiritual awareness in addition to healing. As well as activating our sense of smell, scent molecules are also absorbed through the lungs and skin, and carried all round the body via the bloodstream. This has been known for 2,000 years, thanks to the Greek healer and botanist Theophastrus. Scientific proof has shown that if we boost our 'feel good factor', our immune system is also enhanced, thus keeping infection at bay or, if we do succumb, enabling us to recover more quickly. This means of therapy has been known as far back to when our ancestors were dependent only on the plants and flowers in their immediate environment for tackling disease and injuries. In the 16th century it was Paracelsus' doctrine that said all disease was the result of a person losing touch with his spirituality through corruption of the mind. The obvious cure was to become reconnected with that spirituality.

The writer Johann Wolfgang von Goethe (1749-1832) would have agreed, basing his thoughts in that direction on scientific evidence, backed much later by the beliefs of Rudolph Steiner (1861-1925) that 'the strength of observation and feeling should be believed in and the need to be in contact with the spirituality of nature.'

Early in the last century, the Englishman Dr Edward Bach (1886-1936) noticed that people who were recovering from the same illness did so at varying degrees, even though they were receiving exactly the same treatment. Investigating further, he discovered this was due to the attitude of mind of the individual patient. Those who displayed fear, uncertainty and despair about their situation were likely to make a much slower recovery than those who were more optimistic and positive. From that observation, and with the ancient method of homeopathy in mind, Bach grouped all emotional problems into seven main categories, and with the 38 flower remedies he devised – each being a mixture of a particular flower (usually from the wild), water and brandy – was able to heal the negative aspects of mental imbalance in a patient, thus helping the body to heal itself. For example, Mimulus, or Rock Rose, is recommended for fear; White Chestnut, Clematis, Wild Rose for lethargy; Crab Apple, Star of Bethlehem, Willow for despair. Preparing the remedies is straightforward and is an art that can be learned – under expert tuition, of course.

'That (conserve) of Cowslips doth marvellously strengthen the Braine,
preserveth against Madnesse, against decay of memory,
stopeth Head-ache and most infirmities thereof.'
A Book of Fruit and Flowers
Thomas Jenner

Present-day homeopathy, which has become very popular during recent years, was developed by a German physician Samuel Hahnemann (1755 – 1843), and is a course of treatment based on plant chemicals, not only from the flowers but also the leaves, stem, wood, fruit, bark and roots of plants and trees. These are diluted many times until there are only small traces left. Hahnemann stated that we are all in possession of a life-giving force that normally maintains a healthy equilibrium physically, mentally and spiritually. Illness only shows itself as a symptom of how we are coping with stress: homeopathic remedies help to restore that healthy equilibrium in our bodies. These remedies are usually taken orally by placing small amounts on the tongue, and many such preparations are now available from High Street chemists and health shops.

In Aromatherapy – a very old healing technique going back about 5,000 years – the scents of plants such as clary sage, lavender and rose are utilised. The aromas actually come from oil essences and are steam distilled not only from the flowers but again, from all aspects of plants and trees. These natural chemical compounds are said to be safer to use than pharmaceutical drugs, and are usually applied as a preventative or complementary treatment, mainly by massage, hot and cold compresses, bathing and occasionally by inhalation. They can also be used simply as body scents, or to 'lift' the atmosphere in a room.

Fragrances can have a very deep emotional effect on us, fostering states of reflection and spirituality, or particular states of awareness. Care and consideration are always necessary when planting fragrant flowers in the garden. If particularly strong, too many in a given area can give out an aromatic 'smudge' which can be confusing. So in the garden, powerfully scented plants or flowers are best situated well apart from each other. And it is equally important for us to choose the right flowers when considering our 'garden within'.

They Have a Living Soul - Tehsin Ahmed

I interviewed Tehsin in her gift shop surrounded by beautifully designed wall-hangings, luxuriously-coloured cushions and similar soft furnishings which reflect her Islamic faith.

'The Islamic view of the Garden of Eden is the same as that of Christianity. Likewise, in this life we have two choices given to us. And as a result of the outcome of that choice, regarding the Afterlife, we get sent to Heaven or Hell. Whereas Christianity teaches that Heaven is all white, according to the description of Heaven in the Koran, there are colours very similar to those on Earth, but everything is so serene, more than anything we could have created here. According to Islam, we will find Heaven filled with living plants, trees and flowers we shall only see there, which makes us wonder what else could you see more beautiful than the ones here on Earth? As I respect a fellow-being, I would have the same respect for all things, including all plants and flowers. They have a living soul in the same way as I do.

'If a plant dies, we are not supposed to throw it away, but to bury it so that it will regenerate itself – so with ourselves when we are laid in the earth. The presence of flowers helps to guide us through. Islam teaches us that the purpose of trees, for example, is that not only are they homes to the birds, but provide shelter for us. So if, during a walk I sit under a tree, then I would thank it for letting me rest, the same as I would thank someone for cheering me up with a bunch of flowers. At a wedding, we make necklaces of flowers: these are symbolic of God blessing the happy couple. The colours of flowers and the many different types of flowers are, in a sense, for us to appreciate what God can do for us, and to make us think about the things around us because they are in His image. He is everywhere and in all things. It makes us stay conscious of why we are here.

'Floral images, as on a prayer mat, for example, we look upon as spiritual, although we do not pray to plants. When I pray, or bow down, I do so to God only. We do not do so to any idol, images or pictures. We do not know what God looks like, hence Islamic Art being symbolic of all things in Nature, which is half of what He created. All artwork is an appreciation of Allah – in flowers, or patterns, although there are no human images, no representations of what we think of as God. On a prayer mat there is perhaps scenery, a mosque, Mecca – or a garden.'

Chapter Three

A Land of Fayerye

'Where the bee sucks, there suck I
In a cowslip's bell I lie;
There I couch when the owls do cry.
On the bat's back I do fly
After summer merrily:-
Merrily, merrily I shall live now
Under the blossom that hangs on the bow.'

Ariel's Song – 'The Tempest'
William Shakespeare

Except for wind and sunlight, mention the word 'energy'
relating to the great outdoors and we would normally
associate sound or electricity or both which can be measured
and adjusted. There are other sorts of energy we have to open
ourselves up to if we are to understand phenomena like the
flower spirits – that is, looking deeper, beyond the aesthetics
of shapes and colour. As we know, each flower has its own
characteristics as dictated by its cellular DNA structure, and
its own energy flow, thereby giving access to secret places
within. Instinctively we all have some understanding of
energy flow, although the pace of our everyday lives may have
blunted our awareness of its uses.

While personal energy flows have a bearing on our health,
they can also help us to hone in on the energies of areas like
the flat lands of East Anglia, the Derbyshire Peak District,
the Welsh Mountains, the Alpine meadows of Switzerland,

Appalachian Mountains, the Grand Canyon – or perhaps more familiarly, a favourite coastal resort, local park or secret corner in a wood. But there are other places – our own garden, for example – where the energies may be more subtle, especially when it comes to relating to the flower spirits. We should not consider this as just a 'brain thing', but as something experienced by the entire body.

As we grow up, the 'brain thing' can sometimes pose problems by cluttering our minds with would-be prejudices. The mainstays and beliefs of our early upbringing are, to some extent, discarded as mentioned earlier, but some of us feeling the need secretly continue to harbour those beliefs. We may no longer believe in Santa Claus yet still feel the magic of Christmas. Other concepts – like faeries, especially the flower faeries – have become so interwoven in our folklore over the centuries that even though we may have reached adulthood, and outwardly perhaps dismiss them, there are times when most of us do give them, at least, a surreptitious acknowledgement. The word 'faery' comes from the French 'fee', in turn coming from the Latin 'fatum', from which 'fable' is derived – 'myth' or 'legend'.

We often apply the term 'away with the faeries' to anyone who is considered anything from mildly eccentric to completely mad. But the faeries themselves are anything but mad – though they are certainly mildly eccentric at times! Wanting to see them 'just for laughs' is completely the wrong attitude, held by the wrong sort of people – those who may only superficially 'like Nature', but inwardly feel no inclination to delve deeper. Or those like Myra who just want to keep up with the latest trend.

Possessing an awareness of the spirituality of flowers – of which the faeries are part – is a state of consciousness equal, I think, to a religious experience. And it is said that they are very choosy when it comes to making themselves visible – the ancient Celtic traditions are still rich today, particularly in Ireland.

According to folklore, to say aloud the word 'faery' may have unexpected consequences, for some of these tiny people – of which there are many types – often react unpredictably. Just like us humans, they are not necessarily all sweetness and light. Some are believed to be fallen angels allowed to live on Earth. Some are lost souls with one foot in the grave and the hereafter, and the other one here in the 'visible reality'. However, they do not necessarily represent the nature spirits that we are more familiar with – beings like gnomes, sprites and goblins, so it is said, possess more human characteristics often to the detriment of anyone who may displease them.

Whether or not those in the faery realm do exist is up to the individual to decide. Logic may react negatively, but while I was writing *Living With Ghosts*, someone told me that although they had never consciously experienced anything supernatural, they had nevertheless felt since childhood that there was 'something in it'. I cannot claim to have actually seen flower faeries, yet stubbornly withholding total belief in them because they remain unseen is, I think, to withhold an essential part of innocence and trust – that sparkle of open positivity and purity of knowledge we should strive to maintain for the rest of our lives. Even someone reassessing their negative beliefs may well discover the lost child within.

A faery may be described as a miniature human being, mischievous, with an alert mind and capable of magical powers. To our ancestors, faeries (or 'devas' as they are sometimes called, from the Sanskrit, meaning 'shining one') were part of their visualisation of nature, occupying a vital dimension between the earth and the heavens. The 'little people' of the 'Middle Kingdom' were once regarded as the prime protectors of nature herself – of mountains, forests, rivers and springs – especially the tree faeries and the flower faeries. This was still true of Celtic mythology at the time the Romans invaded Britain.

Faery stories, poems and songs have been passed down orally for hundreds of years. Even Homer included faeries in his *Odyssey* and *Iliad* (850-800 B.C.). Possibly one of the earliest surviving references in English literature comes to us from 1188 when Gerald du Barry, ecclesiastic and writer, travelled through Wales collecting stories from people and including them in his chronicle *Itinerarium Cambriae*. These fairies were described as small, blond and wingless, whereas in ancient Greek art, faeries were shown as tiny human beings with butterfly-type wings.

The Latin name for water-lily, *Nymphea*, from the Greek 'Nymphe' applied not only to the sacred Lotus but also to the many sprites and nymphs found in ancient Greek mythology. By the Middle Ages, they had become faeries, so the water-lily became symbolic of nymphs, faeryland and the abundance of Nature. Around 1200, another writer, Gervase of Tilbury, referred to faeries as 'portunes', describing them as being like little old men, one inch in height, and dressed in shabby clothing, who helped workers till the soil. Obviously their intentions were good – although gnomes, dwarfs and similar types often played adverse roles because of their connection to the underworld. Probably the most famous writer was Geoffrey Chaucer who, in his *Canterbury Tales*, wrote of Britain, when:

'Al was this land fulfild of fayerye.'

In 1485 Sir Thomas Mallory published *Le Morte D'Arthur*, but almost a century later came *Houn of Bordeaux*, also featuring King Arthur, Morgan Le Fey and Oberon, probably the greatest King of the Faeries. It was this source that William Shakespeare referred to when he wrote *A Midsummer Night's Dream*. He also used faeries in his final play *The Tempest*, written in 1611. These little nature spirits continued to inspire many literary efforts throughout the 16th and 17th centuries, although because of the frenetic witch-hunts of the 17th century, anyone who believed in faeries ran the risk of being burned at the stake.

In the 19th century along came the popular faery stories by the Brothers Grimm, and by Hans Christian Anderson. At the beginning of the 20th century J.M. Barrie's *Peter Pan* first appeared and in 1923 Cicely Mary Barker published her first *Flower Faery* book, to considerable public acclaim. Well over 150 poems and wonderful illustrations were to make up what was to become a whole series, each faery resembling the parts of the flower it was supposed to represent. The author wrote that the moment a seed was sown a new flower faery was created, and that these tiny shy beings would appear only to those good children who really believed in them. J.R.R. Tolkein's magical *The Hobbit* and *Lord of the Rings* (the latter having been made into a series of blockbuster films) have enthralled both children and adults alike.

All this still indicates the need we all have for a good faery tale. The German psycho-analyst Louise von Franz considered that faery tale characters reflect the characteristics deeply engrained in our subconscious human behaviour.

Flower Fays and Divas

As we approach the flower faeries, we must consider a story of intrigue and deception. It was in July 1917, at Cottingley, West Yorkshire, that two cousins, Elsie Wright, aged 15, and Frances Griffiths, aged 11, claimed to have actually photographed each other talking to faery folk. Although the pictures were closely scrutinised and declared genuine by some experts, others were very doubtful. The writer Sir Arthur Conan Doyle became totally convinced of their authenticity to the extent that he submitted an article about them to the *Strand Magazine*. Hundreds of readers wrote in to say that they, too, had genuinely seen faeries at the bottom of their gardens. And in 1922, Conan Doyle published a book *The Coming of the Fairies*, based on the Cottingley Faeries. But he was not believed by many and thought to have been completely hoodwinked by the girls.

Sixty-five years later, a journalist discovered some identical pictures of the faeries in an old children's anthology. In 1983, Elsie admitted in an interview in *The Times* that it had all been a hoax. She and Frances had cut out the faeries from a copy of that same anthology, mounted them on cardboard and fixed them to bushes with hat-pins. It seems that Conan Doyle, creator of the world-famous Sherlock Holmes, had been outwitted by those two young girls, after all!

To non-believers of the 'wee folk', the story of the Cottingley Faeries would probably serve as a bench-mark case. But as there are two sides to an argument, an example can always be found to support the opposite point of view.

Martin Colclough is a member of the Spiritualists Union and works as a medium in the Spiritualist Church. Now in his forties, he told me that though as a child he had always believed in faeries (as Nature spirits) and had known of certain places where they dwelt, he had never actually seen any. But recently, while investigating possible methods of contacting them, he performed a meditation and visualisation out-of-doors. This was the result he described to me:

'My wife Nikki and I had got some larkspurs growing in the garden – tall, very attractive, masses of columns of delicate blue flowers. After meditating for some time, I very slowly became aware of a number of tiny faeries busily tending the individual flowers, rather than just hovering around them. My first reaction was that I was going crazy! After my initial surprise, it seemed they were the absolute essence of the flowers. Until then, I had been thinking; "The larkspurs are tall, they'll need support, so I'll have to get some canes." Then I realised they were best left in better, more expert, hands.

'We'd also got some pumpkins, obtrusive plants growing far beyond their allotted area. We should have kept pinching them back but, by then, they were smothered in flowers. I noticed that the faeries attending them appeared to be stocky and strong, more like elves. This was probably because their work was heavier than that undertaken by the larkspur faeries who, by contrast, looked more like traditional faeries – very dainty – and light blue in colour, like their flowers.

'I'm pretty sure the flower faeries are aware of me. Out of hundreds of pumpkin flowers we only got one pumpkin, but as we picked it for Hallowe'en I thanked the flower faeries, because we had only needed one. Even as I was hollowing it out for a lantern, I was sending them a blessing. I can't say they communicate back verbally, so to speak. But our garden is living proof of communication in a way, because when Nikki and I have asked them for help – neither of us being particularly garden-minded – things have grown really well and people have commented on it!

'If you believe in the magic of the faeries, they are there. I think there were sources of magic readily available years ago and the faeries used them for various manifestations. Many people believe those sources no longer exist. But the faeries, in my opinion, still defend that dimension. Such magic hasn't left the world at all. It's just withdrawn into the planet, but it can still be tapped.'

'I know a bank where the wild thyme blows,
Where oxlips and the nodding violet grows,
Quite over-canopied with luscious woodbine,
With sweet musk-roses, and with eglantine;
There sleeps Titania sometime of the night.

Lull'd in these flowers with dances and delight;
And there the snake throws her enamell'd skin,
Weed wide enough to wrap a fairy in.'

A Midsummer Night's Dream
William Shakespeare

Mornings or evenings of stillness, when everything, including ourselves, seems at peace, are the sacred moments, so it is said, when the flower spirits (faeries or devas) may choose to make themselves visible to us – though they continue to perform their flower magic regardless. Witnessing them can give us a greater appreciation of nature and life in general, a greater leaning towards joy and happiness sometimes against the odds and not simply for our own benefit, but to help other people achieve these things too. The flower faeries are basically very happy beings, loving those mortals (ourselves) who are able – with their permission – to communicate with them. Industrious and expert at their job, they are overjoyed if given credit every time we admire the plants or flowers.

A brief mention should be made about their nearest ally – the tree faery. Since earliest times trees were regarded as refuges for the Old Gods and our ancestors were often inspired when sitting under such sources of power. It is said that the young Prince Siddhartha (the Buddha) received enlightenment beneath the Bodhi Tree. According to European folklore, a number of spirits are powerfully connected with trees – the dryads (female spirits of vegetation, who live in trees and fields), for example. They can suffer traumatically if the tree they are attending happens to become damaged in any way. If it is felled, then they will die with it. The hawthorn is reputed to be very magical where the faeries are concerned. They can live in large numbers in any of its hollow branches. Some of them – usually elves – are said to oversee the development of the leaves, trunk and roots, and because it is only one of many types of flowering trees, each blossom is attended by a flower faery.

The flower faeries are said to be attracted by joy and light-heartedness, particularly in some wild corner of the garden where nature abounds. They take on the beautiful colour of their relevant flower (e.g. yellow – wild daffodils; mauve – field scabious). They are said to be drawn to young children which explains why perhaps the young are able to answer questions we grown-ups may ask them about the faery realm.

When we take cut flowers indoors, their attendant faeries go with them. But when they die, some of the faeries will die too, their life-span completed, while others go on to care for other flowers. When a flower dies outdoors, once again some of its faeries die, while others check first that its decomposition has started before moving on, so contributing to the flowers for next season. All rather sad we may think, yet this is the very way of nature, simply following the cycles of death and rebirth.

Now, a word about those ornamental red-hatted gnomes spotted in some gardens. They are usually glimpsed as seated – separately or in pairs – on their toadstools, placed discreetly in some little corner. Some, equipped with fishing rods, may be positioned by the poolside; or en masse they can be seen busily undertaking tasks on someone's front lawn. Feelings of passers-by may vary – if you see what I mean!

These gnomes are believed to have originated in Germany, thanks to Theophrastus Paracelsus, a 16th century alchemist, who believed they were the supreme spirits of nature, capable of living for up to 400 years and inclined to industrious activity around the house and garden – hence their models being equipped with brushes, shovels, spades and wheel-barrows. Others (who have worked hard, no doubt) are portrayed simply mopping their brows with a spotted handkerchief!

A set of twenty-one porcelain gnomes first arrived here during the mid-19th century, to populate a large rockery at Lamport Hall, Northampton, home of one Sir Charles Isham. Many people came to admire them, quickly warming to the idea that they, too, might include such 'charming little characters' in their own gardens. And so gnomophobia took off! But the gardening professionals were not so keen on the idea, and the Royal Horticultural Society actually banned them from its shows. Meanwhile, Sir Charles' daughters, who were not so keen on them either, had the gnomes cleared out as soon as they could. By pure chance, one was overlooked, only to be discovered in the 1990s. By then it was thought to be the oldest of its kind in the world, and was insured for one million pounds.

Whether modern-day pottery or plastic counterparts, readily available in garden centres and supermarkets, have any bearing or not on the spirituality of a place, and its flowers, is debatable. Although, any gnomophile might well say that they do.

As we have already observed, 'conventional thought' – potentially negative baggage from the 'brain thing' – can block our access to the spirit world of Nature and its tremendous sources of energy. Faeries – those strange elementals associated with plant and flower energies – are only experienced when we are in a state of heightened awareness, not through the assistance of drugs, but of pure concentration. It is a state similar to that which we experience each morning and night between sleeping and full consciousness, abandoned yet controlled.

Flowers For Luck and Love

'He loves me, he loves me not.'
Traditional flower petal ritual

Throughout the ages, numerous flower divinations have evolved, enabling a young person to find his or her future partner. For example, in *The Connoiseur* (1755) it was stated that 'if a maiden walks backwards into the garden, without saying a word on Midsummer Eve, and gathers a rose and keeps it in a clean sheet of paper without looking at it till Christmas Day, it will be as fresh as in June. If she do stick it in her bosum, he that is to be her husband will come and take it out.' In Scotland, a young woman with several men interested in her would take a rose leaf for each and scatter them over water. The last one to sink would be that representing her intended.

In 1827, there was an ancient custom still observed in Sutton Bangor, in Wiltshire, whereby flowers were picked – not quite fully opened – and paired, according to the number of courting couples there were in the village. The paired flowers would have initials attached to their stamens and were then secretly stored appropriately, in a hayloft or stable. If, after ten days, one flower entwined itself round its 'partner' it indicated a happy future for the couple concerned. Had it turned away a need for more affection was indicated. If a flower looked faded, this foretold poor health for the partner concerned, while if it died suddenly, death was not far away. If either of the flowers (or better still, both) opened fully, then early offspring was forecast.

Apart from flowers playing a specific part in celebrations or other momentous occasions that punctuate our lives, they have also come to contain special significance regarding our everyday routine.

Derived from the Greek word 'anemos', meaning wind, the flowers of the anemone were once believed to be opened by the wind. Known also as the 'Pasque flower', from an old French word for 'Easter', the anemone also had connections with Adonis. On the occasion when he was gored by a boar, it is said that Venus, the Goddess of love and sexual beauty, shed as many tears as he lost drops of blood. Whereas a rose grew for each of her tears, a blood red anemone is supposed to have grown for each drop of Adonis's blood that was shed. This flower is symbolic either of the soul receptive to a spiritual existence, or the ephemeral beauty of the body.

Bluebells, with their massive blue carpeting of woods during April and May, make an inspiring sight. According to the author Cicely Mary Barker, they have strong connections with the faeries. Known as 'dead-man's bells', however, it is rumoured that if you hear the flower ringing, you are on the verge of death! More positively, their spirituality enhances our confidence and feeling of security, enabling us to share things with others.

Standing for concern and chivalry the bright daffodil, I think, is one of the most welcome sights of spring, whether planted in bowls, beds or 'naturalised' in grassland. As the poet William Wordsworth famously put it:

'I wandered lonely as a cloud
That floats on high o'er vales and hills,
When all at once I saw a crowd,
A host, of golden daffodils,
Beside the lake, beneath the trees
Fluttering and dancing in the breeze.'

Surprisingly, isolated clumps are often seen pushing up through many derelict industrial sites, while original wild daffodils are still found around areas of inland water. In Greek mythology, it was Narcissus who, looking into a pool of water, fell in love with his own reflection and wasted away. The flower having become associated with 'self-love', it also symbolises vanity and indifference to others.

Forget-me-nots represent true love and constancy. On February 29th (Leap Year) two people exchanging posies of this flower means their friendship will be for life. Before he became king, the English Henry IV adopted it as his personal emblem, believing that because whoever wore it would not be forgotten, his followers would remain loyal. Travellers and soldiers would present posies of forget-me-nots to their ladies on departure for foreign lands. Because the flowers of some varieties are curved like a scorpion's tail, it was thought that forget-me-nots were a cure for both scorpion and snake bites.

The foxglove could have acquired its name from the belief that the fox wore a single flower on each foot, enabling it to approach its victim in complete silence. It was also known as 'little people's gloves' because it was thought that the faeries wore them to keep their hands warm. It was variously referred to as 'Faery weed', 'dead men's bellows', 'bloody man's fingers' and 'witch's thimble'. In Scotland, it was deemed unlucky if brought indoors or taken on board ship. Physically it is poisonous and should never be consumed yet spiritually it has healing qualities. Also the chemical digitalin extracted from the flower is used in the medical world as a heart stimulant.

One of the loveliest summer flowers is the heliotrope, noted for its fine light blue or deep purple colour. Its glorious scent gives it the popular name of 'Cherry Pie'. It was said that anyone unfaithful to their marriage vows would find themselves stuck to their pew if there was a bunch of flowering heliotrope in church. Signifying devotion and faithfulness, this beautiful flower was often worn by people in mourning.

Since the ancient Egyptians, lavender flowers have been used in perfumery and in the making of other products of the cosmetic industry. The Romans 'sweetened' the water in their baths with the flowers and put them among clothes to keep them freshly-scented and banish moths. Lavender was also burned on St. John's Eve (23rd June), to keep away witches and 'foul fiends'. In Elizabethan times, it was planted in geometric patterns in knot gardens. Wives used to take bunches indoors to protect themselves from being beaten by their husbands. Among its healing properties, lavender can not only stimulate but calm the nerves (whichever is appropriate). It can restore equilibrium and is excellent for boosting the immune system. Folklore, however, tells us that we should approach the lavender plant with care – there may be a snake hiding under it.

The pure white flowers of lily-of-the-valley are symbolic of purity and chastity. It was for its fine scent that it was grown in monastery gardens and was used against foul smells in the monks' hospital. It was also believed to help ailments such as headache, gout and constipation, though one old alarming belief is that by planting a bed of lily-of-the-valley, you run the gauntlet with death!

There is an ancient superstition that says if you pick a red poppy and a petal falls off into your hand you will be struck by lightning!

The brightness of the marigold, and its long flowering period – from May to the first autumn frosts – made it symbolic of the sun – and a faery flower, though surprisingly, it was also symbolic of grief and despair and was used in funerals. At the same time it was considered helpful in alleviating depression, perfectly understandable going by its cheery countenance and the spirituality it exuded, particularly when viewed *en masse*. Included in herbal remedies, it was used against measles and smallpox. Marigold jam was considered a tasty antidote against witches. In the love stakes, a young woman would pick a flower and place it between her breasts in the hope that it would continue to bloom like the love of the man in her life, while young maidens sometimes mixed the flowers with marjoram and wormwood, simmered them over a fire and rubbed their bodies with the resultant liquid before retiring for the night, hoping they would actually see 'the man of their dreams'.

With its large, double, many-petalled flowers resembling a huge red rose, one of the most beautiful summer flowers in the herbaceous border is the paeony. It is actually a native of Greece and China, where it has rightly earned high esteem. In ancient Greece, it was considered as the original healing plant – right up to the Middle Ages. In China, the exquisite flowers were presented as love tokens in much the same way as forget-me-nots were in Europe. During the Sung Dynasty (approx. 1,000 years ago), the white paeony became very popular, as well as many other varieties. There was also in existence the rare and beautiful yellow paeony. It was reported that the wealthy Chu family grew over sixty thousand plants in their extensive gardens at Yangchow, on the banks of the Yangtze River.

For hundreds of years, Chinese artists have portrayed the flower in many styles, from the simplistic when Buddhism was spreading through the country, to graphic realism approaching photography, to the degree of self-expressionism today that would appeal to tourists. Appropriately, the feminine spirit of the paeony is said to offer us love and sincerity.

Regarding rosemary, there was once an ancient custom whereby mourners carried sprigs at a funeral. Following the burial service, these were cast into the grave. This was still practised as late as the 1870s, particularly at the funerals of the lower and middle classes in the Market Drayton

(Shropshire) area. It was believed to help bring rest to the spirit of the deceased person.

In the mid 17th century it was said that:

'*Rosemary purgeth houses, and a branch of this hung at the entrance of howses drives away devills and contagions of the Plague.*' (Note inconsistent spelling!)

During the 19th century, it was thought that wearing a sprig would grant you success in love and other undertakings, whilst in Devon at the start of the 20th century, sprigs of rosemary were carried in the pocket to enhance the felicity of a couple on their wedding day. It was considered very unlucky should the custom be unobserved. Rosemary growing near to a dwelling, means that the woman of the household is the boss – until the plant dies. Then her husband will be master.

Rosemary was one of the original plants to be used medicinally. Traditionally, it gave protection from evil – it also relieves stress-related illnesses.

Crimson and White

'*Now sleeps the crimson petal,*
Now the white.'

Alfred, Lord Tennyson

Pushing through hard February ground, the charming little snowdrop symbolises hope and consolation, representing Bride, an ancient Celtic goddess who emerged as the days began to lengthen, blessing the people in their homes, who presented her with gifts in exchange. This would be on February 1st, the old Celtic festival Imbolc, also named the Snowdrop Festival, a celebration of renewal, the changing of the Goddess from the Old Crone of Winter to the Young Virgin of Spring. With the arrival of Christianity in Europe, the Celts still worshipped her, changing her name to St. Brigit. February 2nd became Candlemas Day, representing the purification of Mary, the Mother of Christ.

Strangely, although Bride, or Brigit, was welcomed into people's homes, the snowdrop, itself a white flower, was thought to be unlucky if brought into the house, possibly because the shape of this delightful little flower was reminiscent of a shroud. And yet the writer Alison Uttley, recalling her childhood days in Derbyshire, wrote:

'Many things discovered for the first time in the year had the property of bestowing a wish, we said. So off we started, wishing with the first snowdrop we saw, with the first primrose we found, with the first strawberry we ate.'

According to the Victorian language of flowers, the snowdrop is symbolic of high regard.

Some strange beliefs regarding flowers are ancient, while others are of comparatively recent vintage. But like the snowdrop, many other species of white flowers are considered unlucky if brought indoors, even the gloriously sweet-scented lilac – again, particularly the white varieties.

This, too, would apply to the hawthorn (known also as whitethorn or May tree), despite its strong connection to the tree and flower faeries. According to Christian belief, Joseph of Aramathea, on a visit to Glastonbury, England, shortly after Christ's death, pushed his hawthorn staff into the ground whereby it rooted and prospered. This original 'Holy Thorn' was cut down by the Puritans in the 17th century. Its successor is supposed to have been raised from a saved cutting. Flowering at Christmas, as well as in May, it is believed to possess great healing powers.

Rich in folklore, hawthorn blossom is often used during May Day celebrations in the making of garlands and to decorate the Maypole, being symbolic of nature's renewing of life, and sexual union. It has been proved that the berries constitute part of a herbal tonic for heart problems.

All the same, hawthorn was looked upon as a strong omen of death. Children were warned never to take May Blossom into the house or else they would lose their mother.

'Hawthorn bloom and elder flowers
Will fill a house with evil powers.'

Warwickshire saying

The old country people believed the scent of hawthorn flowers was 'like the Great Plague of London'. Although dismissed by some, there is scientific proof to back this claim up. Dying hawthorn flowers actually produce trimethylane, one of the first substances formed when animal tissue begins to decay.

Some people advocate never placing white flowers altogether, saying they will predict death. Similarly, it was thought unlucky for a child to pick up a stray flower that had fallen on the street because they might also pick up a fever.

Flowers should never be taken from the churchyard, whether actually growing or from a vase. Picking a flower from a grave would mean disaster for the family of the person concerned, or his own death within a year. Although red flowers of any sort are thought of as lucky – red is the colour of blood, symbolic of life – to scatter the petals, or leaves, of a red rose on the ground is supposed to predict an early death.

Even to place red and white flowers together in a vase is said to be unlucky, especially if taken into a hospital. This could mean there would be death on the ward - though would be considered perfectly safe to put the red and white in separate vases, or simply add another colour.

Something Extra Special - Pauline Hart

Pauline Hart is a complementary therapist and former nurse. I asked her to give me her thoughts on flower traditions, particularly where they related to hospitals. It's an alarming thought but the way things are heading, might we expect to find real flowers actually banned from the wards in the future? Pauline was reassuring.

'I know that flowering pot-plants have been banned for years, and I recently heard on the radio that there may be a move to ban even cut flowers from hospital wards in case they bring in infection.

'But I think myself that it's something extra special when flowers are brought into a hospital by visitors. The patient always feels the presence of flowers conveys everything positive, not only continued love and respect from visitor or relative, but hope for their own recovery and a better life afterwards. Lovely flowers make it feel comforting also for the staff – although they do have to remove them for the night, because flowers absorb oxygen from the atmosphere during the hours of darkness.

'It's traditionally inappropriate to mix red and white, of course, since they are the equivalent of the Barber's Poll – representing blood and foam – especially not recommended for the surgical ward! And arum lilies are traditionally regarded as funeral flowers, although white flowers are sometimes included in mixed bunches now.

'In maternity wards, the spirituality of flowers is very significant. Not only to welcome the new baby into the world, but to welcome a new mum. She is no longer simply a woman. Even if she is a mum already, the flowers are celebrating the miracle of her becoming a mum once again.'

A Bunch of Lilac

'I was cheered, when from my hospital bed I saw my husband marching up the drive to the main door at visiting time, carrying a huge bunch of lilac. His Mum had picked the lilac out of our garden, and had given them to him to bring to me.

'He tried to sneak them in to me through the window by my bed. But I had never been given flowers before, so I was determined to make the most of it. I smiled sweetly at him, but refused to open the window.

'There was no way out for him. He had to walk through the main door, down the corridor to my ward, and through the watching ranks of women all sitting up in bed.

'He had his revenge though. The flowers were still damp with raindrops, so he shook the blooms all over me, before he conceded defeat and kissed me.

'They were a lovely bunch of flowers, because they were wild and beautiful. And because my husband had brought them to me from home.'

A Rural Pen

Pamela Goodwin

Thoughts of the Gardener

Interlude

During any journey, how good it is to take a welcome break, whether at a wayside café, a services area off the motorway, a seaport or airport. As work progresses in the garden, whether some great estate or your tiny patio with its treasured pots of petunias and pelargoniums, any gardener knows the best moment comes when you can sit down with a mug of tea and enjoy the fruit of your labours.

Such a respite represents an oasis of calm, an essential stopping-off point for body and soul – especially if such a place happens to include a garden! And this is no new idea.

Although the following stanzas from Andrew Marvell's great poem *Thoughts of a Gardener* are an English translation from the Latin in which the poet originally wrote it in the 17th century they still so accurately convey the true spirituality promised by lingering in a garden – quenching the thirst of the soul, offering nourishment for its hunger and providing sheer visual delight.

Thoughts in a Garden

What wondrous life is this I lead!
Ripe apples drop about my head;
The luscious clusters of the vine

Upon my mouth do crush their wine;
The nectarine and curious peach
Into my hands themselves do reach;
Stumbling on melons, as I pass,
Ensnared with flowers, I fall on grass.

Here at the fountain's sliding foot
Or at some fruit-tree's mossy root,
Casting the body's vest aside
My soul into the boughs does glide;
There, like a bird, it sits and sings,
Then whets and claps its silvery wings,
And, till prepared for longer flight,
Waves in its plumes the various light.

How well the skilful gardener drew
Of flowers and herbs this dial new!
Where, from above, the milder sun
Does through a fragrant zodiac run:
And, as it works, th' industrious bee
Computes its time as well as we.
How could such sweet and wholesome hours
Be reckon'd, but with herbs and flowers!

Andrew Marvell

Of course, the garden and its flowers can offer more than nourishment, contemplation and repose to the traveller passing through. It reflects the deeper side of our lives, the peaceful sleep we need to refresh us for the next stage of the journey, the eventual eternal rest to which we all aspire.

During the 1970s, I worked at Trentham Gardens, the now excitingly-renovated extensive grounds of a 'stately home' in North Staffordshire. When they had finished blooming, the spring and summer flower displays would be cleared from the beds, which were then prepared for the following season's plants. As we dug over the ground, we would frequently come across pieces of clay pipes discarded by the gardeners of at least a century before, who used them to smoke tobacco. I like to think that those wise old characters were probably smiling as they watched us. Below our feet, their spirits now nourished and mingled with those of the flowers.

Dead Gardener

rubbing soil from my eyes
I see laughter
and hear youth's heavy feet
stomping sunshine into the earth.

Once, I was a flower.

Paul Gater

Chapter Four

In The Depth of the Flower

'To me the meanest flower that blows can give
Thoughts that do often lie too deep for tears.'
Intimations of Immortality
William Wordsworth

One single flower can hold secrets, wisdom and the knowledge of the universe. My wife Dilys is a teacher of psychic and spiritual development, and she often says that meditating on a flower will make you very aware of its sheer depth of meaning, feeling and power. Whatever you may offer a flower, it will return the gift many times over.

Certain flowers seem to have been singled out as having a profound influence on humanity. The lotus and the rose, through the perfection of their supreme iridescence, the awe and emotion they have aroused, have come to represent within themselves a microcosm of Nirvana, or Paradise here on Earth.

Spirit of the Lotus

A member of the water-lily family, prospering in Egypt, India, China and Japan, its radiating petals are still regarded as symbols of perfection, connected with enlightenment and growing spiritual wisdom. To the ancient Egyptians plants, trees, and especially flowers, were an essential part of everyday life. As with most people, they enjoyed presenting flowers as gifts – both to the living and as offerings up to their dead. Cornflowers, chrysanthemums, jasmine, poppies, irises were all favourites, but pride of place always went to the fabulous blue or white lotus.

In Hermopolis they believed its magic so powerful that at the beginning of the world, the sun was created from a huge lotus bud, floating on primeval waters. A powerful light shone, making the lotus open its petals from which the sun burst forth. At eventide, having moved into the western sky, it returned to the lotus flower which closed up for the night. The next morning, when the petals opened, the sun emerged again, to shine forth on the whole world. As it was of such significance, anyone caught picking a lotus flower without authorisation would undoubtedly have faced harsh punishment. The petals opening were also associated with the female sex organs, symbolic of eternal birth and rebirth.

To the Egyptians the lotus had connection with the sun god Re, occasionally represented as a child lying on a lotus. In Memphis, Lower Egypt, the god Nerfertem was regarded, like the sun, as born of the lotus flower. He is often depicted as a young man wearing an open lotus flower or a crown consisting of a lotus flower, two feathers and two collars, all representing fertility. Either fully open, or even in bud, this incredible flower was often carved on the capitals of Egyptian columns in some of their buildings.

Not only was the flower considered sacred there and in other ancient cultures of the Middle East, but also as far as Mexico. This isn't difficult to understand when this supreme 'Flower of Perfection' emerges pure from mud and water – Man's umbilical cord represented by the long stem, to keep him 'earthed', as much as the fine petals are for the purity and enlightenment to which the human soul may aspire.

The sexual symbolism already referred to has made the lotus the flower most often connected to child-bearing. In China, where having many children was considered highly honourable, this was represented by the image of a small boy holding a lotus. The Chinese not only associated the golden lotus flower with birth and rebirth, but also great wisdom, wealth, happiness and eternal life besides perfection, purity, spiritual awareness and summer ripeness. Figurines of the He-he twin gods, symbolic of prosperity, are depicted carrying lotus flowers in jars as they themselves stand on beds of lotus. The twins have also come to depict harmony and happiness in married couples.

In China, those who lack ideal facilities to grow lotus flowers 'make do' by growing them in large pots of mud and water, placing them in strategic positions round the exterior of their houses. The intensely pink lotus flower is undeniably connected with the changing seasons. The clearness of the lakes and pools of springtime; the leaves emerging in summer, their curving stems actually rising several feet above water level, before developing sacred flowers themselves. On large expanses of water channels were cut through the vegetation, so that people could be conducted by boat, to fully appreciate the blooms in their natural setting.

In India, *padma* is the Sanskrit for Lotus, being pure beauty and holiness. In Hindu temples, various objects of worship, some as small as a scent shaker, can be found in the form of a perfumed lotus flower, symbol of creation. A 3rd century figurine of the mother goddess squatting in childbirth has a lotus flower for a head, embodying fertility. And in Indian miniatures Krishna, an incarnation of Vishnu – embodying divine love – is often shown presenting the flower to Radha, his love. Meanwhile the 1000-petalled lotus represents divine birth as Brahma, the Hindu creator god, emerges from the navel of Vishnu, his avatar, while seated on a lotus, about to create the universe.

To Buddhists, purity and primordial waters are from which all life was originally created. At the birth of the Buddha, it is said that the bud of a lotus opened and he stepped into the flower, staring in ten directions – so it became a symbol of the Buddha's own personality and he is often depicted as being enthroned on a fully-opened 1000-petalled lotus flower, representing Nirvana as well as resurrection, life, hope and eternal joy. In Tantric Buddhism, the stem and blossoming of this lotus represents a masculine-feminine image of both sexual and spiritual harmony. On a banner in a Tibetan sacred temple, lotus flowers may be shown offering protection, surrounding the Buddha's halo.

Buddhism is a philosophy based on compassion, charity and non-violence, and the lotus radiates all these things.

Spirit of the Rose

To the Egyptians, Greeks and Romans the rose, with its exquisite scent, was sacred, its reputation further enhanced as a potion for the inducement of love. And like the lotus, in Persian and Islamic gardens, it was symbolically very important. According to legend, it was in the Great Garden of Persia that the rose was created by the first rays of the rising sun. Whilst on the one hand, the moon has always represented the eternity of beauty, flowers have symbolised its poignant brevity. Our human life span has often been depicted by flowers in still life paintings, particularly in the 16th and 17th centuries, where a rose shedding its petals indicates our own vulnerability, or shows us the fragility of owning a surfeit of worldly goods.

The significance of flowers is, however, generally associated with youth, beauty and happiness. For centuries they have been recognised tokens of love, both spiritual and sensual and remain the most appropriate representatives of love, epitomising its freshness and spontaneity. Whether fine bouquets or just posies, all are especially welcome as Valentine tokens.

The word 'posy' itself is derived from the word 'poesy', which means a poem or motto of love.

'What's in a name? That which we call a rose
By any other name would smell as sweet.'

Romeo and Juliet
William Shakespeare

There does appear to be some magic in the name, though. We have all heard of the ballet *Spectre de la Rose*, but why not have it called, say, *Spectre de la Honeysuckle*? Too many syllables clutter the title, but that's not the whole story. The rose, due to its super sensual qualities, has always had an extra powerful link with romance, far more so than the honeysuckle flower, though this too has its own romantic connections, according to the French.

For the Romans, the rose and its scent had particular associations with Venus, their goddess of love and sexual beauty. The ancient Greeks knew her as Aphrodite, and regularly filled her temples with masses of roses.

Bion of Smyrna, (circa 100BC), a Greek poet, recounted the love story of Venus and Adonis. The fact that when her love was killed, the goddess wept tears that became glorious roses is surely an example of how flowers – of whatever kind - can help ease the pain of bereavement purely by the spirituality of their presence. They are transformational, making life more bearable, though physically they don't change anything. Simply by being there, flowers seem to work gentle magic. Perhaps that is the reason why the Romans scattered roses on their graves, not only to signify the shortness of mortality, but also to acknowledge the possibility of continuing life in the Beyond.

In Roman times, rose petals had many uses. At banquets they were dropped into the wine, as an antidote for drunkenness. Women used them as face packs, to reduce signs of ageing. Returning armies paraded victoriously through streets strewn with rose petals. It is even said that the Egyptian queen, Cleopatra, ordered a room to be filled knee-deep in rose petals, in the hope of seducing Mark Anthony! Two people less fortunate, were smothered to death during an orgy held by the Roman Emperor Heliogabalus (204-222 A.D.), renowned for his debauchery: they were buried beneath tons of rose petals released from the ceiling of the high chamber. Later, the Saxons threw red and white rose petals, representing the passion and union of a couple during their wedding ceremony.

The intense power and beauty of the rose down the ages has endowed it as a worthy symbol of birth, rebirth and eternal life. The emblem of the Cabbalistic Society of the Rosicrucians is of the rose situated at the heart of the Cross, the heart of Christ, the Divine Light at the pivot of the Wheel of Life.

It was during the 13th century in France, that rose windows first appeared – great panels of stained glass, depicting masses of roses, and sometimes roses within roses, all radiating from a central point. They represented both human aspiration and enlightenment, and their attainment, via a geometric perfection of form. Symbolising eternity, one of the most beautiful early examples was the West Rose window in Rheims Cathedral, known as the Litany of the Virgin Mary.

The rose was considered as sacred by both the ancient Egyptians and Greeks, despite their similarly shared feelings regarding the lotus flower. With Aphrodite still in mind, the rose too is symbolic of all aspects of Womanhood, its beauty, purity, even holiness. Christians saw it – of course - as an attribute to Mary, the mother of Christ, which was how the word rosary, or rosarium, (meaning Rose Garden) came into use. The word 'rosary' also referred to the crown of roses worn by statues of Mary as well as the chaplet used to keep account of each incantation of the "Hail, Mary". In fact the 'rosary' is what the prayer is now called while counting the beads, similar to the way Hindu and Buddhist monks recite their own liturgical texts, hymns and mantras.

The incredible red rose, because of its vital importance in the work of the mediaeval alchemists, was known as 'The Rose of the Alchemists.' The red rose in particular, is important to many esoteric traditions the world over while in Christianity, it is said that a red rose grew from each drop of Christ's blood that fell as he hung on the Cross. Mary, his mother, is often painted holding a red rose in her hand. It is considered the flower of great passion, its velvet-like petals and stem of sharp thorns, forming a symbol of duality – the ecstacies and the agonies of participants in their sometimes difficult journey in finding that perfect oneness which pure love can bring – so attaining a certain balance of opposites.

As any florist will tell you, every aspiring lover prefers to send his love red roses in the hope of encouraging worldly romance. Pop songs down the years have echoed Robert Burns, who romantically declared:

'O, my luve's like a red, red rose
That's newly sprung in June.'

The power, attraction and spirituality of the yellow rose is symbolically used to represent the State of Texas in the United States of America. In quite a different connection, there was a papal decree in the mid 18th century, creating the Order of the Golden Rose, to be conferred upon women Catholic rulers. Surprisingly, this rose also stands for infidelity in the 'flower code' used in courtship by the Victorians. For a young lady to be sent a bunch of yellow roses was to indicate that her suitor was jealous of someone else.

The clarity and, at the same time, delicate mystique of the white rose has made it the perfect representative of the Moon and of the light. For a Victorian suitor to present a bouquet of white roses to his intended was an expression of total respect for her youthful purity. This rose has traditionally always symbolised charm, purity, virginity – and secrecy!

It was believed that a rose suspended over the dinner table demanded that all confidential talk, whether of business, love, or even scandal, should remain undisclosed outside the walls of the room. The expression 'sub rosa' ('under the rose') explains the once fashionable central rose we often see on ceilings dating from the Victorian era.

Surprisingly, many people still regard this stunning emblem of passion as something quintessentially 'English'! One or two species of roses actually are, but many are native to a vast area - from Europe, across to Persia and well into Asia. When the Romans came to Britain, they brought the exquisitely perfumed Gallica rose. This proved a great favourite for hundreds of years, especially with the Victorians, who also enjoyed the white, musk, damask rose, moss or cabbage roses, and their own recently introduced Bourbon rose – all very much appreciated and still planted, today. Crusaders of the 12th and 13th centuries returning home to England from their military campaigns in the Middle East were tough and merciless, but also deeply intrigued by the magic of the rose – they were to bring back with them a number of fine species.

By the 1950s there were many hundreds of varieties of hybrid-tea roses listed in nursery catalogues, their evocative names including 'Peace', 'Pink Peace', 'Elizabeth of Glamis', 'Chinatown' and 'Blue Moon'. When I was training at Horticultural College, these became extremely fashionable, together with the multiflowering florabundas – everyone wanting lots of colour, following years of austerity. With the appearance of Graham Stuart Thomas's book *Old Shrub*

Roses, however, people were urged to rediscover the colour and fragrance of the original species of roses while the 1960s saw nurseryman David Austin producing roses with something like the scent and shape of the 'old-fashioned' kind, yet with the repeated flowering ability of the hybrid-teas.

During my career, I planted some of these for various clients and was able to assess the results. I did feel that the new varieties represented a very welcome development. Even so, given the choice, I believe that many thinking gardeners would still be drawn, for example, towards our own ancient, wild native rose of the hedgerows – the Sweet Briar or Eglantine, with its superb fragrance and clear pink flowers. And the reason? The iridescence and the spirits are believed to be so much stronger in such an original, unsullied flower.

Spirit of the Wild

'To see a world in a Grain of Sand,
And a Heaven in a Wild Flower,
Hold Infinity in the palm of your hand,
And Eternity in an hour.'

William Blake

Our wonderful wild flowers in their masses, once glorified woods, meadows and hedgerows in profusion. Flowers like red campion, corncockle harebell, foxglove, ox-eye daisy, poppy, primrose, pansy, ragged robin, violet and many others once grew relatively without mankind's interference. They were enjoyed on the simplest level by the ordinary people, and inspired the country's visionary composers, artists and poets to produce some of their very best work.

I can remember a particularly special field near my home. Every spring it was carpeted with masses of pink lady's smock, while at the bottom end, which was more moist, there grew a large expanse of bright, shiny yellow king cup or marsh marigold. It seemed that the whole area would take on an aura of mysticism and magic for the villagers who, for many generations, had always visited the site during those particular months. In the late 1950s, however, the adjacent country road was upgraded to connect with the near-completed M6 Motorway and the lower end of the field was sold off, and drained to become the site for a service station. Ultimately, houses were built on the rest of the field, as well as on several others.

The history of our magical British wildflowers reads like some exciting saga, beginning about 15,000 to 20,000 years ago at the retreat of the last Ice Age. Glaciers had covered much of Northern Europe and no living plants had survived, except on mountain tops above the ice and along some coastal areas, where plantains and sea campion grew; Arctic and tundra vegetation had prospered south of the Thames, beyond the ice sheets.

With so much water still contained in the ice, Britain was connected to Ireland and the Continent. As the climate improved, conifer forests spread northwards, succeeded later by deciduous forests – except for the north of Scotland, where parts of ancient pine woods can still be found today. Meanwhile plants and flowers had time to spread freely from the milder Continent. By about 5,000 years, they had formed the basis of our present wildflower population.

As the sea-level rose, Britain was cut off from the Continent, so no more migrations of vegetation took place. And then Neolithic Man arrived around 3,000 B.C., with his flocks of animals, grain and stone axes - mankind began to make an impact on the environment, continuing to do so right through to the present day.

So many magical and spiritual wildflower habitats suffered during World War Two, when almost every available field and meadow – whether clay or chalk land (often supporting rare species of orchid) – even some parks and large gardens - were turned over to produce as much home-grown food as possible. Few, if any, of the original sites were ever 'returned to the wild'. In his excellent book *How To Make A Wildlife Garden* (1986), Chris Baines stated that by that date, the nation had lost 95 per cent of wildlife meadows. Hundreds of miles of hedgerows – some ancient - have been grubbed too, making way for prairie-style farming.

'If there were nothing else to trouble us,
the fate of the flowers would make us sad.'
Aphorisms and Reflections
John Lancaster Spalding

Have we lost the treasures we took so much for granted? Have the wild flowers and their intense spirituality gone for ever? This would indeed be something to regret.

The former practice (which I can remember during my boyhood) of cutting hay for winter fodder meant that plenty of wild flower seed remained in the fields, to germinate the following year. Some sites had remained undisturbed since medieval times, so had built up a considerable legacy of wild flowers. But when 'new, improved' strains of commercial grass seed were introduced, they were ploughed annually, prior to sowing, while the widespread use of herbicides from the mid 1950s onwards meant any wild flowers that did survive were killed off chemically, leaving only the 'new' grass to mature. 'Clean' cereal crops meant fields – and prairies - of monolith cropping. Hayfields speckled with corncockle, or cornfields with shades of red poppies became almost sights of the past.

The wheel has turned full circle, and it is the derelict industrial waste lands that often provide alternative sites for our wild flowers, today – including the 'less favoured' species like hedge mustard, common ragwort, rosebay willow-herb, nettle, dock and pineappleweed. Daintier, prettier flowers flourish there too, all offering a glorious supportive background for an immediate, important wildlife scenario. Garden escapees like cotoneasters, buddleias, lupins and honesty do the same.

"But why should we conserve wild flowers in the first place," you may ask, "if they're simply a reminder of the way things were? That's just sentimentality."

To me, there is absolutely no question about this. Apart from their colour, beauty and spirituality, the wild flowers have been a part of a countryside that has evolved over thousands of years, expressive of the bounty and harmony of nature. When man stepped in – making some mistakes along the way because he thought he knew better – it was the gentle instruction of the wild that taught him to respect nature and all it stood for. By the 1950s, the countryside had been decimated in the name of profit – every acre became a production statistic, whether it was for the number of cattle or sheep raised, or the amount of grain, oil-seed rape, linseed or softwood timber that could be achieved there. Everything in the natural order - including our bird life, small wild creatures and native wild flowers, bereft of some aspect of their individual habitats - suffered as a consequence.

Our wild flowers know better than we do about what they need. We have seen how the spirits of each blossom will tend it without interference. Many are extremely choosy regarding the right conditions for their growth and prosperity, such as soil acidity, rainfall, sunlight, shade, wind, moorland and coastal exposure - human intervention into any of these factors can be catastrophic. Our wild flowers are part of the food chain, supporting the caterpillars of various butterflies and moths, also insects for the bird life to feed on, their seed another source of food for the birds. There are sound scientific reasons for the conservation of wild flowers: although the healing properties of many have been known, some for centuries, there is always the possibility that revolutionary new cures for serious illnesses may be discovered.

'Tonight from deeps of loneliness I wake in wistful wonder
To a sudden sense of brightness, an immanence of blue -
O are there bluebells swaying in the shadowy coppice yonder,
Shriven with the dawning and the dew?'

Bluebells
Lucia C. Markham

During the 1970s, various botanists and horticulturists, like Daisy Lloyd at Great Dixter, in East Sussex and the scientist Miriam Rothchild at her home, Ashton Wold, in Northamptonshire, were conducting experiments in the planting of flower meadows.

When Miriam Rothchild died in January 2005, aged 96, according to Katherine Swift writing in *The Times*, the lawns at Ashton Wold 'were replaced by long grass and native wildflowers. "I do not much care for living on a snooker table," Rothchild once said. 'Weeds' (self-sown foxgloves and poppies and ox-eye daisies) lapped right up to the windowsills. The vegetable garden blazed with ragwort and harebells...her garden was the product of a passionate commitment to wildflowers and creatures of every sort.'

More landowners, including Prince Charles at Highgrove, in Gloucestershire, support the various organisations actively devoted to reintroducing the wonder, strength and diversity of the wild flowers, not only with regard to meadows – but woodland, mountainside and coastal sites, too. Cities like

Sheffield have wild flower meadows in their parks, while some local authorities sow or plant swathes of wild flowers along motorway and roadside verges, where they can easily be appreciated by the hard pressed motorist. even at a passing glance.

Living in the Staffordshire Moorlands, I was delighted to hear recently that the Staffordshire Wildlife Trust has declared an old landfill site as one of the most 'biodiverse' in the county. The owners Lafarge Cement UK, had used the site for disposing rubble and cement waste until the end of 2003. Previously closed parts of the site had been covered with soil and planted with trees, but in the remaining area, the firm decided to simply let nature take its course – with the result that a recent survey has now shown the ex-landfill site to be in the top 3% of areas rich in plant-life in the county. 73 different plant species – including the common spotted orchid and trefoils – having been identified, together with a variety of bent and fescue grasses.

I'm glad to say that with our own gardens we are in a position, to 'give back' to nature, especially as our homes are probably built on sites of former woods and fields. Even in a city, small individual gardens added together can be the equivalent of a considerable area of open space. In large urban gardens the total number of trees, shrubs, plants and flowers form a valuable asset not only to the vital bird population, but for bats, hedgehogs, insects – even the odd fox or two. And if every garden owner devoted a corner to wild flowers that would add up to having a small wild flower meadow in the vicinity.

To grow wild flowers has become much simpler for the potential enthusiast, over the past few years. 'Big name' seed firms now offer mixed packets, stocked by garden centres, some of which may have young plants on offer for those people who haven't time to raise them themselves. Many first class gardening books available have useful sections devoted to the cultivation of wild flowers, or deal specifically with the intriguing subject itself.

Some time ago, I raised from seed some cowslip and wild primrose plants, which I planted in groups on a low bank by a stream in a garden belonging to two friends of mine - with a wonderful beech wood as a backdrop, and a source of dappled sunlight. Within a couple of years, self-sown seed produced from the resultant flowers had germinated enough to almost cover that area of the bank with more new plants and, consequently, with yet more flowers.

My two friends have both since said that that whole area of the garden now feels so different when the bank is in full bloom. Although they weren't any more specific, I think I knew what they meant.

Sources of Ancient Magic - Dilys Gater

My wife Dilys Gater has worked for over ten years as a psychic, medium and healer. Her books about her work are read world-wide.

'The natural forces are always there, whether people believe in them or not. We need to learn a little humility when dealing with them. Regarding any kind of natural energy though, it is a lot less complicated than we think. It doesn't matter whether we say we appreciate the flowers or not, the flower spirits are always positive. No way can they be otherwise.

'You can't dictate to nature. Not mixing red and white flowers, for instance – where did that come from? If you investigate nature's resources, you can find actual red and white on the flowers themselves – old roses like the so-called Tudor Rose, or variegated carnations with red and white petals. All these beautiful things were hugely powerful, sources of ancient magic. Nature teaches us. Her spirits are all-powerful, always there, and there is no way you can destroy that incredibly magnificent energy.'

'Flower in the crannied wall,
I pluck you out of the crannies:-
Hold you here, root and all, in my hand.
Little flower – but if I could understand
What you are, root and all, and all in all
I should know what God and man is.'

Alfred, Lord Tennyson

Chapter Five

Days of Wine and Roses

'Flowers have an expression of countenance
as much as men or animals.
Some seem to smile; some have a sad expression;
Some are pensive and diffident;
others again are plain, honest and upright,
like the broad-faced sunflower and the hollyhock.'
A Discourse on Flowers
Henry Ward Beecher

Life is all about moving on in the subtle presence of the flower spirits. In order to guide us, they may manifest themselves in different forms – physically, or in the vast realms of folklore, sometimes in dreams. They alleviate the dark night of the soul, speak to us meaningfully – they give us all the answers, providing we know how to decode what they have to say.

We often say we 'dream of retiring' to somewhere with a garden. It is an ideal, symbolic of achievement, rest, peace well-earned. There is a Chinese proverb that says: 'If you want to be happy for an hour, get drunk. If you want to be happy for a year, take a wife. But if you want to be happy for eternity, be a gardener.' The flower spirits help us celebrate high days and holidays, but they also offer us day-to-day counsel and wise advice.

Experts say that when we dream of a garden, whether we may know it or not, its condition will reveal much about our characters as well as our past, present and future. If neat, well-kept but with hardly any flowers, our life should be fairly comfortable, apart from one or two minor upsets. A really beautiful garden in full bloom indicates a wonderful life of domestic harmony, financial security, love and continuing spiritual development. A neglected garden in our dreams warns of adversity, loss of peace of mind and love.

In the west we look on gardens as expressions of perseverance, development and spiritual growth. In the Middle East dreaming of gardens also symbolises the 'finer' parts of Woman – and making love - especially if the dreamer is eating fruit! Somewhere or another, as it inevitably does in life, love creeps in! In Victorian England, a young girl who visualised a garden full of vegetables in her sleep would be blessed with a happy marriage – while a young man dreaming of a garden of pretty flowers, was being urged to pursue the young lady of his desires with renewed vigour.

Dreaming of fresh, brightly coloured flowers of any kind growing outdoors or indoors, foretells a personal life of great happiness. If the flowers happen to be dead or dying, or if you discard them, you are being warned against being over-confident and careless. To dream of wearing a beautiful garland of flowers indicates a victory over adversity and being given a garland means similar progress, but if you are offering a garland to someone else, it is a warning that you are putting too much trust in other people.

Dreaming of wild flowers is an expression of the freedom of the woods and fields of life, a happy, glorious prospect. Any kind of artificial flowers in our dreams though, send out a warning to be on our guard against betraying our hard won principles.

The miracle of spring occurs annually, and we never tire of witnessing the emerging glory of its flowers. One of the pleasures of wandering in the gardens of our dreams is that our favourite flowers can appear there at any time of the year, whatever their actual season. As we slumber, we can enjoy a bouquet of the most unlikely hothouse flowers mixed with alpines, and glorious exotics glowing alongside plants from an English water meadow.

The anemone appearing in our dreams has very wide potential – it highlights spiritual aspiration but also carnal desire! To dream of a bank of beautiful azaleas in full bloom is indicative of impending good news regarding money. The crocus, an early reminder of spring, appropriately indicates approaching opportunities, urging us to discard old regrets, while daffodils suggest we forget our worries and cares. Whether growing in the garden or elsewhere, dreaming about them signifies a long and happy life ahead. It's a similar story with narcissi – growing in the garden, they depict joy for the future. Growing in pots indoors in our dreams, however, they also offer a subtle warning against being arrogant and overconfident. The lovely little jonquil is supposed to depict an extremely passionate sex life!

Hyacinths, growing in the open, suggest unexpected happenings ahead. Whether good or bad, we have to be prepared to face them, but if we dream of them in pots, things are going to get a lot better. Strangely enough, planting tulips in a dream foretells possible disappointment - seeing them in flower or picking them, is a much happier portent. A late spring candidate is the very spiritual hawthorn flower, which reassures the dreamer positive devel-opments are on the way. It is also indicative of protection, a happy marriage or a forthcoming birth. To dream about primroses (for me the true representative of spring), is said to forecast a passionate, but tempestuous love affair either for someone we know or for ourselves.

Dream of wearing a beautiful blue gentian as a button-hole and you will attract true love and nurture long-standing friendships. To see these flowers growing indicates a life of simple pleasures. Another blue/purple flower, the exotically-scented heliotrope, suggests to its dreamer a satisfactory love life and security both spiritual and material. Heather means something slightly different in that everything around us is well blessed, especially if it is white heather, dreamt with the sun shining on it. That straggler the sweet-scented honeysuckle, bestows love on the single man or woman in their dreams, and also offers the likelihood of domestic happiness and opportunities in the business world.

A rapid rise in one's social status is indicated in a dream about lilies, while lily-of-the-valley promises contentment and happiness in both home life and love affairs. By contrast, pansies hint at unpleasantness, even a quarrel. I find this surprising, since they normally convey a great deal of long-lasting charm and beauty both to the heart and to the spiritual vision of the 'third eye'.

A paeony in our dreams can indicate stress and anxiety, while a popular candidate for mass bedding and hanging baskets, the petunia, reveals that enjoyable times are on the way – maybe a holiday. Poppies in our dreams, especially yellow ones, offer us the possibility of sheer sensual delight, but red ones suggest we keep control of our temper.

To dream of the sunflower warns us against voicing our opinion and behaving impulsively, unless in the company of those we can trust. If in our dream we are actually eating the seeds of this flower, an old friend is about to return. Further warnings may come in the shape of the water lily, emphatic that we should not over reach ourselves, but restrict our ambitions what we know we can do. Dreaming of the evocative wisteria that normally scrambles up the house wall – with its pinnate leaves and lengthy racemes of blue, mauve, white or pink flowers – suggests success in love and domestic bliss, but hints of a need to step back from a relationship that has gone wrong for awhile.

The Language of Love

'Flowers are Love's truest language; they betray,
Like the diving rods of Marigold,
Where precious wealth lies buried, not of gold,
But love – strong love, that never can decay!'

Park Benjamin

On their wedding day, the newly married couple are traditionally sent on their way amid a fanfare of joy and celebration from their friends and relatives. They are empowered by the loving presence of flowers that on such an occasion are regarded as equally as significant as the religious aspects of the occasion.

Particular flowers included in wedding bouquets are often chosen for their symbolic meaning, in addition to their colour and scent. A mixture can often be interpreted as having two or more meanings – for instance, red roses and orange blossom together represent happiness, passionate love and fertility.

BLUEBELL - constancy.

BLUE VIOLET – innocence and faithfulness.

CARNATION – uniqueness.

DAISY – pure innocence.

FORGET-ME-NOT – absolute love.

80

GARDENIA – joy, happiness.

LILY – purity.

LILY-OF-THE-VALLEY – truth and happiness.

MAGNOLIA – dignity, pomp and circumstance.

ROSEMARY – commitment and loyalty.

ORANGE BLOSSOM – happiness, fertility.

RED ROSE – passion.

WHITE ROSE – purity.

RED AND WHITE ROSES – together forever.

Colour and flowers are equally important to the followers of Islam. At a Buddhist wedding, for example, following the marriage vows it is customary for the couple to not only light incense sticks together but to offer a gift of the most beautiful flowers to the image of Buddha, specially set up for the joyous occasion.

Garlands, too, are symbols of joy, celebration, and blessing. In the South Sea Islands, visitors are welcomed by having garlands put around their necks by the inhabitants. At the end of October, it is customary, in Papeete, Tahiti, to have parades of floats, richly decorated with flowers. The Polynesian emblem is the tiare flower, snowy white in colour and with a fine scent. This is used in garlands and woven into the hair, and has its own festival joyfully celebrated during the first two days in December.

In Northern India, before a Hindu wedding, the groom goes to the house of his bride, proudly mounted on a fine horse. His ceremonial garb usually consists of a long brocade or silk tunic – or a western suit! In either case he will be wearing exquisite garlands of flowers, while in Southern India a bride wears a superbly embroidered silk sari, usually of gold and covered in jewellery, besides being richly garlanded with flowers. Our every encounter with flowers stirs our awareness of the blessings the flower spirits imbue in our souls. We are filled with energy and well-being, our own celebrations radiating out happiness towards others.

'...all I longed for was one common flower
Fed by soft mists and rainy English air,
A flower that knew the woods, the leafless bower
The wet, green moss, the hedges sharp and bare –
A flower that spoke my language, and could tell
Of all the woods and ways my heart remembers well.

Then came your violets – and at once I heard
The sparrows chatter on the dripping eaves
The full stream's babbling inarticulate word,
The plash of rain on big wet ivy leaves;
I saw the woods where thick the dead leaves lie,
And smelt the fresh earth's scent – the scent of memory.'

'Winter Violets'
Edith Nesbit

Prior to the written word, our ancestors gave flowers to each other, not necessarily for their beauty, but for their symbolism. Like the well dressing ceremonies, this tradition goes back to pagan times in Britain, when flowers were believed to voice the messages of the old deities. In the same sense of sacred communication, early Christian monks dedicated some flowers to the saints.

For hundreds of years, throughout periods of both war and peace, the language of flowers continued to be 'spoken'. In the Middle Ages and after, flowers were picked from cottage gardens, or even from the woods, fields and hedgerows and given rural names to indicate sincerity, flirting and even infidelity. Their blooms were presented as love tokens as young lovers walked out together. The Victorians, however, evolved a more contrived code in which particular flowers, used in the pursuit of one's intended, conveyed very specific meanings.

APPLE BLOSSOM	-	'You are definitely my intended.'
BLUEBELL	-	'I can be both patient and faithful.'
CARNATION	-	'I hold you in very high esteem.' Once called 'coronations', and were worn as coronets or chaplets by the rich on special occasions. Also applied to pinks, flowering at the same time.
CARNATION (PINK)	-	'I am a woman deeply in love.'
CARNATION (RED)	-	'I am giving you my heart.'
CARNATION (STRIPED)	-	'No! Well, yes!'
CHRYSANTHEMUM (RED)	-	'Here is my everything.'
DAISY	-	'All my trust in you.'

FORGET-ME-NOT	-	'Truly yours.'
HAWTHORN BLOSSOM	-	'All my love and trust.'
LOVE-LIES-BLEEDING	-	'Pure love.'
ORANGE BLOSSOM	-	'I love and respect you.'
PANSY (WILD)	-	'Love in vain!' Shakespeare originally referred to this flower as 'Love-in Idleness'.
SWEET WILLIAM	-	'I love you, believe me!' In Gerard's *Herbal* (1597), the author says that they are 'best esteemed for their beauty, to deck up gardens, the bosoms of the beautiful, and for garlands and crowns of pleasure.'

It was the poet Rupert Brooke who referred, rather surprisingly, to the tulip as being the English 'unofficial rose'. The tulip actually takes its name from the old Persian word for 'turban', because of the close resemblance of the flower to that particular item of headwear. The country of origin was Turkey and it was during the early part of the 17th century that tulips were brought to Europe via Holland. There the demand became so great that a huge escalation in their value took place and they became almost priceless - then the inevitable happened, fortunes having been both made and lost. In the language of flowers, the tulip has come to depict feminine respect and intuition.

TULIP (RED)	-	'Truly, my declaration of love!'
TULIP (YELLOW)	-	'Helplessly in love.'
TULIP (VARIEGATED)	-	'What wonderful eyes.'

Roses appear everywhere, their beauty and symbolism depicted in numerous paintings, including Redoute's exquisite series of *Roses*, and the famous one by Botticelli which shows the Virgin Mary kneeling with the Infant Christ in an enclosed rose garden, depicting Divine Love. It was during the 19th century that roses in particular became extensively used to convey coded messages. They had a language of their own, even to the degree in which they were cut and presented.

ROSES	-	'Love, nothing else but love.'
ROSES (YELLOW)	-	'I am jealous.'
ROSES (WHITE)	-	'Worthy of your purity and love.'
ROSES (RED & WHITE MIXED)	-	'Together – double my love.'
A RED ROSE BUD	-	'You are lovely and pure.'
A FULL BLOOM PLACED OVER TWO BUDS	-	'Our secret!'
A CLUSTER OF MUSK ROSES	-	'I truly think you're charming!'
A ROSEBUD WITH LEAVES & THORNS	-	'I have my doubts, but live in hope.'

A MOSS ROSE	-	'Utter love.'
A WITHERED RED ROSE	-	'Our love is over. I'd rather die!'
A RUGOSA ROSE	-	'Your only asset is beauty.'

Picking roses in a dream is supposed to foretell great happiness and joy, especially to a young woman, for an offer of marriage isn't too far away. To receive a bunch of roses means success on the social scene – business conferences, parties, meeting people and making new friends. To give roses to someone signifies that you are loved and appreciated, both physically and spiritually. Dreaming of artificial roses, however, can be interpreted as possible jealousy and deceit regarding a close friend; so too withered roses imply deceit on the part of a loved one, while white roses are believed to be portents of illness. To dream of red roses, to the Victorians especially, symbolised honour and vitality.

Flower Power

So flowers accompany us through the courtship, the wedding and the secrets of marriage and childbirth. Even the labour of childbirth itself – as well as its transcendental joys – is accompanied by the subtle presence of flowers. At various times, there have been fashions of naming children after flowers, most of these being girls, since the flowers are traditionally a powerful realm of femininity.

Flower names may come and go but they never quite disappear. The Victorians loved them and the flowers have had several 'revivals' since then, while some names may not be so obviously connected with flowers, but all possess their symbolic invocation.

ANTHEA	-	representing a flower.
ANTONIA	-	flowering, flourishing well.
BLOSSOM	-	abundance, zest for life.
BRONWEN	-	white blossom.
CARMEN	-	a garden of paradise.
DAISY	-	joy, bliss, feeling of completion. Fidelity, possible association with faery lore.
FLORA	-	fertility. She was the Goddess of spring, flowers, fruit and vine. Festivals held in her honour were usually wild occasions!
HEATHER/ERICA	-	connecting with other people. Steadfastness. Erica is the Latin word for heather.
IRIS	-	embodiment of perfection.
JASMINE	-	emotional stirrer through scent.
LILY	-	peace within. It is said this flower was given to Clovis, King of the Franks, by an angel, when he adopted Christianity in 496 A.D.

MARIGOLD	-	associated with healing power. Also mediator between two sides in an argument.
PANSY	-	of love. Sometimes referred to as 'Cupid's Face'.
POPPY	-	joy, positivity, abundance. Bringing out the best in oneself and others, but with the possibility of being vulnerable at the same time.
PRIMROSE	-	possessing the spirit of love; the joy of spring's awakening.
ROSALIE	-	an abundance of roses.
ROSE	-	pure in spirit, calming.
ROSEMARY	-	similarly aligned to purity of spirit.
VIOLET	-	to promote companionship.

Interestingly, I came across only one masculine 'flower name':

BASIL	-	affiliated with the balance of life; the happy medium in thought and action.

During the Victorian era the use of flowers, in decoration, whether indoors or out, was the dictate of the lady of the house. It was Mrs Beeton who prescribed particular flowers to adorn the dining table at different times of the day – bowls of rose buds and forget-me-nots at lunch time; roses and vivid red pelargoniums in the evening. Settings for opulent parties were enhanced by flowering climbers over arches, and banks of potted *flora exotica* were lavishly arranged against a background of ferns and palms – all conservatory and hot-house grown thanks to the expertise of the gardening staff.

Young women were encouraged to wear flowers in their hair, read books on, and practice flower fortune telling, engage in flower embroidery, draw and paint flowers from life. Flowers being viewed as symbols of love and romance it was sometimes suggested that the young daughters of the house in particular (and sometimes those considered to have been 'left on the shelf'), should equip themselves with pen and paper, and pass the time 'doodling' images of favourite blossoms. The rose always proved to be a definite winner – an indication that love was sorely needed. It was said that young ladies with a pronounced maternal instinct tended to choose other kinds of flowers!

There are also rhymes in which flowers have also come to depict true love. For example, this old rhyme for Valentine's Day:

'Lilies are white, diddle, diddle.
Rosemary's green.
When you are King, diddle, diddle.
I will be Queen.'

There are many versions. Perhaps the most widely known is the one that became the basis for a pop song, some years ago.

'Roses are red, dilly, dilly.
Lavender's blue.
If you will have me, dilly, dilly,
I will have you.'

Another very well known rhyme, although nothing to do with love, was one most of us learned in our infancy, singing it as we held hands with friends, forming a ring, and then falling onto the ground at the end of it.

'Ring-a-ring o'roses,
A pocket full of posies,
A-tishoo! A-tishoo!
We all fall down.'

This is thought to date back to days of the Great Plague. It was believed that a rosy red rash was a symptom of the disease, while posies of herbs or flowers, were carried by people concealed within their clothing, in an effort to protect themselves. Sneezing was recognised as symptomatic of one of the later stages of infection, the final line speaking for itself.

It is claimed that art of dried and silk flower arranging has widely increased as the quality of commercially produced 'drieds' has vastly improved over recent years. Much stronger and truer to original colour and form, they are now more easily available through outlets like florists, specialist shops and garden centres. Many dedicatees create arrangements from the effectively simple to the intriguingly involved, attempting to connect with the spirituality of the real thing. The same is also said about silk flowers – enthusiasts even claim they can be substituted into an arrangement of fresh flowers with hardly anyone noticing.

Artificial flowers may appear to 'lift' a place where there are no genuine flowers, as part of the décor in a busy department store, say, or even in a corner at home, helped by discreet lighting. They can also look most attractive on a stage set in the theatre, though on display in a florist's shop, they cannot compete with the glorious presence of the real thing.

But whether dried flowers or even pressed flowers – the latter often seen collected and collated in old albums – they have been 'stopped' from achieving their full life-cycle as intended by nature. To me, the spirituality has been drained from them – the flower spirits have either departed or been killed off, leaving a feeling only of sadness. To me, all dried or artificial flowers are technically dead, possessing either a stagnant energy or no energy at all – especially when their colours begin to fade and they gather dust.

I asked Marion Boon, a former lecturer in horticulture who is now a 'nursery person', whether artificial flowers held the same magic as real ones for her.

'I don't feel that there is any spirituality at all regarding artificial flowers, no matter how much they look like the real thing,' she said. 'They do not have a consistency of natural, growing material. With genuine flowers, even if they are only in bud, you get the scent or aroma of the foliage (look at the chrysanthemum, for example). When you go into the greenhouse you can always pick up on the spirituality of the plants and flowers. They are living things.'

A Different Sort of Seeing - Ian and Alice

I was once involved in the planning and construction of a garden specifically for blind and partially sighted people to enjoy. From a technical point of view, this involved building raised beds in brick – it would be too easy to stumble if there was no clearly defined path.

Up-ended lengths of concrete piping were firmly fixed into the ground to form a series of separate urns, while the area was surrounded by tall rustic trellis against which scented and interestingly textured climbers were trained. The strongly perfumed plants included selections of honeysuckle and roses (but roses with few, if any, thorns), summer jasmine and various ivies.

The raised beds and concrete urns were filled with good compost and planted up with a wide choice of plants, flowers, aromatic herbs and shrubs. We chose textured flower and leaf surfaces rather than beautiful blooms, as the partially sighted would obtain far more sensory pleasure from touch than colour. The plants were also chosen to establish themselves quickly. A particular favourite was the aubretia, while the perennial candytuft and various thymes soon spread and softened the hard, straight edges of the beds and urns.

Interestingly though, it was not until Dilys and I played host recently to Ian Rattray and Alice Crick, two friends in their early forties, both from London, that I really appreciated how very differently a person must view flowers and their spirituality if unable to see them. Ian is registered as blind, while Alice describes herself as being visually impaired. I asked them to give me their impressions of 'viewing' flowers purely through the sensations of touch and scent.

They seemed to find it difficult to express their feelings. Ian reported that touching flowers evoked a sense of male or female, according to texture – whether the plant felt coarse or very silky. He was slightly nervous of plants if they were at all spiky, and because he could not make associations between image and flower in the same way as a sighted person, he had a fresh and interesting view of scent.

'Despite what people say about lilies being sweet,' he told me, 'I don't like the smell. I find lilies very acidic.'

Alice commented that when she tried to look directly at a flower, it 'seemed to disappear into itself', so for her just a sideways glimpse was best. But she said she loved flowers and their scents, and always felt in strong communication with the flower spirits.

Chapter Six

A Garden For All Seasons

'Observe the circling year, how unperceiv'd
Her seasons change! behold! By slow degrees,
Stern winter turn'd into a ruder spring;
The ripen'd spring a milder summer glows;
Departing summer sheds Pomona's store;
And aged autumn brews the winter storm.'

'The Seasons'
John Armstrong

Creating a flower garden, whether from scratch or from the remnants of a previous one – or even maintaining an existing one – inevitably involves a certain degree of physical graft. There is no way of avoiding the hard labour, but if approached in a positive way, this work can represent the energising and harnessing of spiritual energies, those of the emergent garden and our own, resulting very much in the well being of both. A symbiosis – a focus is created.

To our ancient forbears it was the fire at the entrance of their cave which provided that focus. Later, the hearth, the fireside in our homes assumed the role. The family would gather round the bright flames to share and discuss their various experiences of the day. Nowadays, such a family focus has been partially dissipated – parents sit downstairs watching television, their offspring retire to their rooms, each with a television of their own as well as their computers – and there isn't even a hearth any more. Central heating has seen to that.

Communication within society as well as within the family unit has become minimalised as a result, so we especially need the loving assistance and partnership of the flower spirits as times grow ever more fragmented.

The garden provides a wonderful source of sustenance and enrichment. Like a favourite sofa by the fireside, its appealing familiarity grows ever stronger with each encounter. The worries and brickbats of daily survival can seriously deplete our own spiritual energies – we need that daily 'fix' among the flowers, the most positive and beneficial sort of dependency there is, continuing to build up that powerful trust between ourselves and them.

During the early years of my horticultural career - thanks perhaps to Tom, my 'spirit friend' from childhood - I was always aware of something mysterious beyond the obvious, visible only through the 'third eye'. The achieving of maturity and awareness was a gradual process over the years. I was already conscious of the spirituality and nobility of trees and shrubs, so perhaps it should have been a swift and obvious step to begin appreciating the spirituality of the flowers - especially as trees and shrubs are themselves bearers of flowers. But maturity unfolds at its own pace in the same way as time which, according to our perception of it, appears to 'drag' when we are young yet catapults us through the seasons the more we achieve that wholeness of maturity.

In this chapter I would like to share with you some of my personal reflections with regard to tending a flower garden through the year, from the coldest months to the hottest, from the highest days of summer to the quiet of winter where the cycle of the natural world turns slowly back to resume the process all over again.

Spring

'For snowdrops are the harbingers of Spring,
A sort of link between dumb life and light,
Freshness preserved amid all withering,
Bloom in the midst of grey and frosty blight,
Pale Stars that gladden Nature's dreary night!'

'Harbingers of Spring'
Caroline Elizabeth Norton

As the days become longer and the sun a little stronger, one of the most exciting things for me is to take an early morning walk round the garden and feel the wonderful surge of energy and excitement generated by the flowering plants, the hopeful strength of bulbs pushing up through the surface of the still cold earth. With the renewed swell of birdsong too, it always gives me a really positive sense of rebirth, both physically and mentally.

Throughout his long life Igor Stravinsky remembered with awe the cracking of the thick ice as the clear waters began to pour forth, everything exploding into almost savage growth whenever the severe Russian winters of his early years relented. This eventually became the idea for his ballet *Le Sacre du Printemps*, in which a young virgin is ritualistically sacrificed to the pagan gods in thanks by her people for their survival throughout the darkness of winter to the unfurling of the new season.

As we enter the new equinox we may still encounter a dramatic phase or two of wintry weather. But as things start to settle there is a sense of relaxation and expectancy. We may become very 'garden conscious' in our different ways – ranging from cheerful prospects of a fresh season of plant-ordering and nursery visits to the more mundane promise of 'another year's chore of lawn-mowing and hedge-cutting.'

When I was self-employed, most of my clients took a very personal interest in their gardens. As with my own, the idea for all of us was that the garden should not 'stand still' but continue to evolve – though always, of course, with the welfare of the flowers and fauna in mind. In the same way as a very positive garden, a stagnant one too, I always feel, will reflect the attitude of its owner.

There is much to be recommended in taking time getting to know the individual plants, trees and shrubs in one's garden. I have always looked upon mine as great friends – a very practical and spiritual relationship having been built up between us over the years.

Although some of my clients regularly dispensed with my services at the end of October – mainly because their gardens were so small there was little for me to do – I would return in mid-March. I would feel a sense of real pleasure in discovering that someone's greenhouse or conservatory contained trays or pots of young seedlings, almost ready for pricking out, rather than simply the discarded plants from the house, or even a dead Christmas tree! Here was an investment in the future, an optimistic looking forward, a gesture of sharing - it was like reconnecting with a welcoming friend.

A routine job I always enjoy during March is pruning roses, and any shrubs I have neglected to do the previous month. Many gardeners simply get on with the task without thinking about it, but there are others of more discernment who, although they achieve the job just as quickly, actually 'ask' the subjects concerned for permission to carry out the job. They may not speak out loud, but frame the request inwardly all the same. And what is wrong with this? After all, we often hold conversations with ourselves, managing to arrive at the logical answer to our problem as a result.

97

I don't think it should be a case of 'the poor old shrub' having no other option. The understanding practitioner will sense immediately that the flower spirits (or devas) have given him their trust to accomplish that task. The same procedure applies too throughout the different seasons – when the right time comes, say, to divide clumps of polyanthus, monarda, oriental poppies or golden rod; to prune, or even move, a tree; to prick out seedlings, cut back Virginia creeper, plant out tender annuals, or 'disbud' chrysanthemums.

Martin Colclough, who told us earlier in the book how he encountered the flower faeries, mentioned something else that recently happened in his garden.

'I had to move four Chamaecyparis conifers, last year. After I'd moved the first one, Nikki, my wife said: "Did you tell it you were going to move it?"

'"Oh, yes," I lied. "No problem!"

'Well, after that I made a point of telling the other three that I was going to transplant them to a better situation in the garden. The beauty of it was, they survived and are prospering well. But the first one died. There must definitely be some truth in the old saying - if you talk to the spirit of the plant, it does seem to work.

'Nikki likes to have roses for the house so I always thank the bushes for providing the flowers for the vase. It's just like what the American Indians used to do. If they wanted bark for a canoe, they used to thank the tree for the bark. When they killed a deer, at the first cut they thanked it for providing meat, and the spirit of the deer went into the Great Beyond.'

Summer

'Had I a garden, it should lie
All smiling to the sun,
And after bird and butterfly
Children should romp and run,
Filling their little laps with flowers,
The air with shout and song,
While golden-crests in guelder bowers
Rippled the whole day long.'

'Had I a Garden'
Alfred Austin

Summer, of course, is the richest season, holding an absolute wealth of flowers to its name. Traditionally, the summer months mean long hours spent drowsing in the sun and the scent of a beautiful garden. Although from my point of view, it is rarely like this for the busy gardener!

During the summer it is likely we will be far more closely involved with the flowers in our garden – and perhaps with other people too – than during the rest of the year. Everyone enjoys coming out of doors on a sunny afternoon or evening; we see neighbours' bobbing their heads over the hedge or fence; there is a sense of enjoyment and camaraderie as we are perhaps invited to look at the gardens of friends, or even sit and share a traditional cup of tea, or a long cool drink in the shade.

As I look round my own garden, I can see that there is the summer bedding to be planted, there are gaps to be filled in the herbaceous border with the relevant plants and, similarly, the shrub beds need to be tended. Oh, and of course, I must not forget to keep everything watered when necessary, stake the dahlias, put supports to the burgeoning sweet peas and constantly dead-head spent flowers such as ageratums, begonias, fuchsias and roses (to name only a few), so that many more beautiful blooms will come in their place as the season moves on. I try to plan ahead too. By establishing the odd choice tree or two (planted out from containers), I like to think I'm providing something not just for the summer, but also for the longer term.

'Gardening requires lots of water – most of it in the form of perspiration.'

Atlanta Journal and Constitution
Lou Erickson

Surprisingly, some people tell me that although they enjoy gardening they hesitate at the thought of getting their hands 'dirty'! Any true gardener will tell you that it is by getting soil on your hands that you feel the urgency to get things done. A bit of grubbing in the ground is the best way to achieve that sense of freedom and the reassurance of being in touch with Mother Earth.

For me, the most magical time in the garden is at night.

During the day, the sun-drenched flower borders burst into a riotous, yet silent song of colour, joined by the blackbirds, sparrows, robins and linnets – whose songs are very much heard. Add to this the distinctive buzzing of insects, their manic circular flight forming haloes over groups of white regal lilies. Nature is providing a chorus of approval, perhaps.

I suppose we might sometimes think of ourselves as solely responsible for creating a beautiful garden. The natural world, however, has a way of teaching us our place in such matters. After labouring under a relentless sun, tired and covered in perspiration, the gardener can sometimes long for that unexpected bout of thunder, sudden burst of wind or shower of heavy rain to clear the air. When it comes, as we dash scrambling through the mud for shelter, we become very aware that this same beneficent natural world is very much testing the mettle of her 'merrie tillers' of the soil.

Working in a garden of absolute perfection, there would be very little to do, so we can welcome the storms. We need to be confronted by that constant grounding challenge, in the same way as in other aspects of our everyday lives. What really matters is to be in possession of the knowledge of how to cope.

Following the summer storm, I retie some of the plants, cut away broken shoots, tend the damaged flowers as best as possible, gather up their fallen leaves and shattered petals. At the same time, my spirits are lifted on seeing the many flowers that remain undamaged despite the downpour and dashing wind. It is then, following this ritual of regular challenge, that I feel the garden and its flower spirits may be regarding each one of us as their true - if continually tested - partner. This has to be our best reward.

And there is a spot of precious free time after all – time to be able to walk barefoot across the grass, to sit down, relax and absorb the beauty, inspiration and profound feelings of peace that emanate from the particular flowers of our choice. Time to reconnect with their delicate and lovely spirits.

Autumn

'O Autumn, laden with fruit, and stained
With the blood of the grape, pass not, but sit
Beneath my shady roof; there thou may'st rest
And tune thy jolly voice to my fresh pipe,
And all the daughters of the year shall dance!
Sing now the lusty song of fruit and flowers…'

'To Autumn'

William Blake

I think that unlike the spring, this is the season that really prompts us to work hard, nudging us – however gently it might try to do so - into renewed physical energy. In autumn there is inevitably plenty of activity. Think of the seasonal flowers – autumn crocuses on the rockery or planted to bloom among the shrubs; Japanese anemones, masses of border chrysanthemums, groups of Golden rod and Michaelmas daisies, red hot pokers, blazing clumps of yellow, orange or red rudbeckias, heleniums, together with Kaffir lilies. All these rally us, cheering us through to the grimmer prospect of facing another winter.

Dahlias, geraniums and heliotropes – leftovers (till the first frosts) from summer – these also contribute, though perhaps a little sadly, to the show. Their bright colours may be dimmed, the blossoms tainted now by the damp, shortening days, in spite of the warm soil.

The dank smell of initial decay throughout our fields, woods and gardens puts us in touch with feelings of destiny. It is the time of year when we may begin to realise that, although flowers are the principal residents of a garden, their overall effect on us is subtly enhanced by the presence of fine foliage plants, shrubs and trees. The thoughtful gardener should not just be concerned with colour, but with form and architecture. Expressions of these can range from the various ornamental grasses to mahonias, conifers (of various shapes) and hollies – to name just a few. Many come into their best – either for their flowering, foliage effect or berries – during autumn and into winter.

It may be obvious by now that after the flowers, my favourite source of colour is that offered so fantastically by the autumn leaves of our trees. For me there is little to beat an English woodland at its best - though I do regret not being more widely travelled sometimes. For instance, I can appreciate only intuitively by way of photographs and movies the incredible show of emblazoned leaf colour seen each fall in New England, U.S.A.

102

Some years ago, at the bottom of the garden, I decided to plant a number of Japanese acers on a site sheltered from the wind and direct sunlight by tall privet hedging. During every autumn since, their brilliant display of leaf colours has become more and more spectacular. It was as a student that I first became 'switched on' to autumn colour, following a visit to the Westonbirt Arboretum, in Gloucestershire. There (and in other such centres) you will see that all kinds of effects can be created in the autumn garden – from the subdued to the bright and brash. The prospect is worth consideration for the autumn gardener, perhaps employing coloured bark effects, seedheads, numerous berries and, of course, always, especially the flowers.

So now in my own garden, the summer bedding is removed and composted, the beds are prepared for forget-me-nots, winter-flowering pansies, bellis perennis, wallflowers and the many bulbs to be planted. It is also a time to take stock of the season just past - to start thinking about any alterations that need to be done around the garden.

Holding on to tried and trusted friends in the flower border is fair enough, but I always encourage gardeners to try out something new, whether a simple, straightforward change or relatively more difficult. It is the challenge that matters - and we gardeners should not be afraid of celebrating the feeling of success where it is due. If I have successfully raised some uncommon primulas or lilies, from seed, I will always quietly thank the resulting plants for responding so favourably to my efforts.

Winter

When icicles hang by the wall,
And Dick, the shepherd, blows his nail,
And Tom bears logs into the hall,
And milk comes frozen home in pail,
When blood is nipp'd and ways be foul,
Then nightly sings the staring owl,
Tu-who;
Tu-whit, tu-who – a merry note,
While greasy Joan doth keel the pot.

Love's Labour's Lost
William Shakespeare

An old gardener I knew once remarked that everybody's garden looked the same in the snow. But we still notice and appreciate the individuality of the flowers as they push through their white wintry overblanket which nowadays, tends to thaw within a short time of falling. There they are, the small yellow aconites, the snowdrops, crocuses, small irises blissfully unaware and, one of my true favourites, the early daffodil, the dazzling variety 'February Gold'.

When the weather restricts us indoors, what better prospect than to gaze out through the window on a drift of winter-flowering heathers; or, by contrast, appreciate the brightness of those many small yellow flowers on the Winter Jasmine as it scrambles up against a dramatic dark backdrop of yew? There can be absolutely no shortage of form or colour in the winter garden – just see the daphne, the mahonias, skimmias, winter sweet, witch hazels and many more.

The flower spirits, with their willingness to lift our own, are always there. And we can feel our positive response helps them to benefit in return, even in the cold.

For me, one of the richest things about gardening is to experience the fascination and joy of a really hard and frosty morning. With the sun low in the bright blue sky, it illuminates the frozen masses of delicately-skeined spiders' webs that stretch right over and along the holly hedge. The herbaceous border, with its dehydrated Michaelmas daisies, golden rod and plumes of pampass grass is held in a frozen frieze, dusted as though with icing sugar. Globe thistles petrified in white offer a tremendous sight too, as does Sedum spectabile, its flat, now mummified, red/pink panicles now transformed from the magnets that attracted the late summer and autumn butterflies.

One of the best and most beautiful garden trees I can recommend, flowering intermittently between November and March, is the so-called Autumn Cherry. Its semi double white, or pink, flowers will bring a sense of real joy to any dull winter's day. I was amazed to learn that seeing this tree in flower in a dream is supposed to indicate approaching death - not a physical one, I hasten to add, but the ending of a period or situation in life that will be followed by one more spiritually enriched. We all have our individual ways of arriving at such significant turning points – but reflection on the deep wisdom of the Autumn Cherry is perhaps an appropriate thought at the ending of the old year and the start of the new.

I always think one of the most important jobs to get finished is the winter digging, allowing the cold weather sufficient time to save a lot of work for us later on – by breaking down those clods of newly-turned soil, especially if they consist of heavy clay. Digging may not be the favourite job of most gardening enthusiasts, and I think everyone will agree with Charles Dudley Warner (1829-1900), author of *My Summer in a Garden*, who stated:

'What a man needs in gardening is a cast iron back, with a hinge in it.'

I have always considered myself a 'winter person', and I do find digging rewarding and exhilarating, especially on a very cold, crisp day. To take care of that 'cast iron back', the secret is not to overload the spade. It is a job that I have learned to delegate to 'auto-pilot': while I am working I can concentrate on other things, perhaps deciding which new varieties of particular flowers I might try, selecting from the crop of newly-arrived catalogues through the post. This is also a great opportunity to see where plants will go on the site in question, in relation to their different heights and flower colour.

But the true blessings of the garden mean there is treasure to be found always. We do not need to wait until another season, but can relate to what we see at out feet. I remember one particular late winter's afternoon, working in the garden of one of my clients. In the gathering dusk, with the pleasurable anticipation of time relaxing with some new CDs of the classical music I love (the operas of Richard Wagner, actually), I was thinking about returning home. Even with a hot evening meal and the warmth of a fire beckoning several miles away I hesitated, a knife-edged breeze blowing the first snowflakes of a threatening blizzard into my face.

Suddenly I noticed the plant at my feet, finding myself gazing in wonderment at the dark, newly opened flowers of a helleborus, hardly visible as they bent their heads to the ground. I stooped down and, with thumb and forefinger, gently drew one of them up. Looking straight into the flower, in my *Parsifal* frame-of-mind, perhaps it was then that I caught just a glimpse of my own, personal Holy Grail. I felt I had been given a gift for the new season that lay ahead, just a moment with that little flower and I was wiser and more spiritually enriched.

'And time remembered is grief forgotten,
And frosts are slain and flowers begotten,
And in green underwood and cover
Blossom by blossom the spring begins.'

Atalanta in Calydon
Algernon Charles Swinburne

A selection of other titles from Capall Bann

Flower Wisdom - The definitive guidebook to the myth, magic and mystery of flowers by Katherine Kear

From the poppies of Flanders - symbols of sleep and oblivion - to the purity of the lily and the faery associations of the daisy, flowers have always been surrounded by myths, magic and mystery. This illustrated guide explores the physical and symbolic properties of the best known and loved flowers of the Western hemisphere, including the bluebell, lily, anemone, poppy, daffodil, iris, rose, and many others. Each flower is described in terms of its botanical properties, its origins, the folk-lore and history that surrounds it, and how it is used for health and well-being. All plants are inextricably linked to the science, culture, religion and economics of the world. Some are used to heal, others become symbols for worship, others a trading commodity or status symbol, Flowers can indicate political allegiance, romantic passion, sympathy and social class. They are universal symbols of ephemerability and purity, and of the natural cycles of birth, death and regeneration. Packed with a wealth of information, this is a unique guide to the myth, magic and wisdom of flowers. ISBN 186163 237 1 £14.95

Reflections From Beyond   Jeannie H. Judd and Geoff Hamilton

An account of a remarkable contact between the spiritual and physical dimensions. Everything moves on, in the etheric world too; Geoff Hamilton's great love of plants has led him to study them there in much greater depth, producing surprising results that can benefit our physical lives if we follow his gardening suggestions in part one. Geoff and Jeannie, another keen gardener, teach the benefits of working with plants on a vibrational level, with garden plans that work on specific colour vibrations or with specific plant groups to enhance healing, meditation and/or health. Section two contains further knowledge, concerns about harm being caused to our planet and the urgent need to halt the damage and restore the natural balance of the Earth. Also contains several of Geoff's entertaining significant fables and tales. ISBN 186163 147 2   £8.95

Wondrous Land - The Faery Faith of Ireland   Kay Mullin

"....a delight...a living, personal story from the Atlantic edge..." 3rd Stone

Dr Kay Mullin, a clinical psychologist by profession, was introduced to the world of faery by spirit channelled through a medium. That meeting led to extensive research in Ireland, collecting stories both old and new - from people who not only know of faeries, but see them too - in the land so long associated with them. The result is this wonderful book. The text is complemented with lyrical poetry from an Irish seer, and exquisite drawings. The faery faith is real, alive and growing in Ireland. Illustrated by Cormac Figgis. ISBN 186163 010 7 £10.95

Real Fairies   David Tame

"Here we have first-hand accounts....reliable witnesses....Highly recommended!"

The Cauldron *"sure to be of interest'* The Fairy Ring   *"a fascinating read"* Silver Wheel

Encounters with fairies seem to be increasing. This book relates the experiences of many people, some famous (such as BBC presenter Valerie Singleton), some clairvoyant, some everyday, who have seen and met members of the fairy kingdom. It appears that our world and theirs are drawing closer together again and it is possible for more and more people to see real fairies. ISBN 186163 0719 £9.95

The Urban Shaman by Dilys Gater

We do not all need the wide open spaces of the country to find the spiritual awareness of the shaman within ourselves; it is not even necessary to long to 'get away' from the city. You carry the sacred space and the doorways into the Otherworlds within your own head, wherever you are. Although born and bred in the Welsh countryside, Dilys loved her ten year stay in London where her spiritual and psychic development progressed against the backdrop of the bustle of city life. London pigeons, police horses and city cats and dogs are just as relevant and as valuable as white owls and golden eagles, she says. For some people the 'quiet' of the countryside is essential, but for others it is an uncomfortable environment - if you are one of these, this book will appeal, inform and teach. ISBN 186163 2274   £11.95

Can't Sleep, Won't Sleep - Insomnia, Reasons and Remedies
by Linda Louisa Dell

This book gives some of the many reasons for sleep problems and sets out some of the many remedies, therapies and techniques that can help you to re-train your sleep patterns to your very individual needs. Starting with an explanation of what insomnia is, the author progresses to cover the purposes of sleep, dreaming, sleep posture, depression, chronic fatigue, women's problems, stress, SAD, relaxation techniques, hands-on healing, and much much more. Problems and possible remedies are blended here making fascinating reading and a real help for anyone experiencing sleep problems - and so many of us have for all sorts of reasons. Help yourself get a good night's sleep - read this! ISBN 186163 238X   £13.95

Magical Guardians - Exploring the Spirit and Nature of Trees
Philip Heselton

"*..shows us that the trees in our gardens, parks and woods have a spiritual nature. Highly recommended.*" Prediction "*deals with trees as wise and sentient beings we can communicate with by contacting their inner energy...Highly recommended*" The Cauldron This is a book about trees, but a book with a difference, for it acknowledges trees to be wise beings who can teach us much if we approach them in the right way. This book shows how to go about it, revealing the origins of our awakening interest in - and love for - trees. Trees have a spiritual nature, and opening up to this spirit has been a constant feature in human society. Through practical guidance, this book gives hints on how we can make that contact for ourselves. The personalities of the ancient trees - our Magical Guardians - are explored, and the book reveals how we can start to acquire some of their deeper meanings. ISBN 1 86163 057 3   £12.95

Places of Pilgrimage and Healing   Adrian Cooper

"*Very moving and very informative...a very rare book...Never have I read such a compelling and instructive book...provides a lot of answers...A brilliant book....Writing of rare distinction...Very Highly recommended*" BOL.com. The 45 people interviewed in this book had all been told by mainstream medicine that there was "no hope" for their medical, psychological and spiritual conditions. Each of them has a powerful story to tell which defies the orthodox prognosis that they received. They were drawn from all around the world and tell inspirational, practical, insightful, compassionate, wise, patient, gritty and breathtaking tales of their personal pilgrimages. These are stories for a world in need of healing. ISBN 186163 0883   £13.95

FREE DETAILED CATALOGUE

Capall Bann is owned and run by people actively involved in many of the areas in which we publish. A detailed illustrated catalogue is available on request, SAE or International Postal Coupon appreciated. **Titles can be ordered direct from Capall Bann, post free in the UK** (cheque or PO with order) or from good bookshops and specialist outlets.

A Breath Behind Time, Terri Hector
A Soul is Born by Eleyna Williamson
Angels and Goddesses - Celtic Christianity & Paganism, M. Howard
The Art of Conversation With the Genius Loci, Barry Patterson
Arthur - The Legend Unveiled, C Johnson & E Lung
Astrology The Inner Eye - A Guide in Everyday Language, E Smith
Auguries and Omens - The Magical Lore of Birds, Yvonne Aburrow
Asyniur - Womens Mysteries in the Northern Tradition, S McGrath
Beginnings - Geomancy, Builder's Rites & Electional Astrology in the
    European Tradition, Nigel Pennick
Between Earth and Sky, Julia Day
Book of the Veil , Peter Paddon
The Book of Seidr, Runic John
Caer Sidhe - Celtic Astrology and Astronomy, Michael Bayley
Call of the Horned Piper, Nigel Jackson
Can't Sleep, Won't Sleep, Linga Louisa Dell
Carnival of the Animals, Gregor Lamb
Cat's Company, Ann Walker
Celtic Faery Shamanism, Catrin James
Celtic Faery Shamanism - The Wisdom of the Otherworld, Catrin James
Celtic Lore & Druidic Ritual, Rhiannon Ryall
Celtic Sacrifice - Pre Christian Ritual & Religion, Marion Pearce
Celtic Saints and the Glastonbury Zodiac, Mary Caine
Circle and the Square, Jack Gale
Come Back To Life, Jenny Smedley
Compleat Vampyre - The Vampyre Shaman, Nigel Jackson
Creating Form From the Mist - The Wisdom of Women in Celtic Myth and
    Culture, Lynne Sinclair-Wood
Crystal Clear - A Guide to Quartz Crystal, Jennifer Dent
Crystal Doorways, Simon & Sue Lilly
Crossing the Borderlines - Guising, Masking & Ritual Animal Disguise in the
    European Tradition, Nigel Pennick

110

Dragons of the West, Nigel Pennick
Earth Dance - A Year of Pagan Rituals, Jan Brodie
Earth Harmony - Places of Power, Holiness & Healing, Nigel Pennick
Earth Magic, Margaret McArthur
Egyptian Animals - Guardians & Gateways of the Gods, Akkadia Ford
Eildon Tree (The) Romany Language & Lore, Michael Hoadley
Enchanted Forest - The Magical Lore of Trees, Yvonne Aburrow
Eternal Priestess, Sage Weston
Eternally Yours Faithfully, Roy Radford & Evelyn Gregory
Everything You Always Wanted To Know About Your Body, But So Far
    Nobody's Been Able To Tell You, Chris Thomas & D Baker
Experiencing the Green Man, Rob Hardy & Teresa Moorey
Face of the Deep - Healing Body & Soul, Penny Allen
Fairies and Nature Spirits, Teresa Moorey
Fairies in the Irish Tradition, Molly Gowen
Familiars - Animal Powers of Britain, Anna Franklin
Flower Wisdom, Katherine Kear
Fool's First Steps, (The) Chris Thomas
Forest Paths - Tree Divination, Brian Harrison, Ill. S. Rouse
From Past to Future Life, Dr Roger Webber
Gardening For Wildlife Ron Wilson
God Year, The, Nigel Pennick & Helen Field
Goddess on the Cross, Dr George Young
Goddess Year, The, Nigel Pennick & Helen Field
Goddesses, Guardians & Groves, Jack Gale
Handbook For Pagan Healers, Liz Joan
Handbook of Fairies, Ronan Coghlan
Healing Book, The, Chris Thomas and Diane Baker
Healing Homes, Jennifer Dent
Healing Journeys, Paul Williamson
Healing Stones, Sue Philips
Herb Craft - Shamanic & Ritual Use of Herbs, Lavender & Franklin
Hidden Heritage - Exploring Ancient Essex, Terry Johnson
Hub of the Wheel, Skytoucher
In and Out the Windows, Dilys Gator
In Search of Herne the Hunter, Eric Fitch
In Search of the Green Man, Peter Hill
Inner Celtia, Alan Richardson & David Annwn
Inner Mysteries of the Goths, Nigel Pennick
Inner Space Workbook - Develop Thru Tarot, C Summers & J Vayne
Intuitive Journey, Ann Walker Isis - African Queen, Akkadia Ford
Journey Home, The, Chris Thomas
Kecks, Keddles & Kesh - Celtic Lang & The Cog Almanac, Bayley
Language of the Psycards, Berenice
Legend of Robin Hood, The, Richard Rutherford-Moore
Lid Off the Cauldron, Patricia Crowther

Light From the Shadows - Modern Traditional Witchcraft, Gwyn
Living Tarot, Ann Walker
Lore of the Sacred Horse, Marion Davies
Lost Lands & Sunken Cities (2nd ed.), Nigel Pennick
Magic For the Next 1,000 Years, Jack Gale
Magic of Herbs - A Complete Home Herbal, Rhiannon Ryall
Magical Guardians - Exploring the Spirit and Nature of Trees, Philip Heselton
Magical History of the Horse, Janet Farrar & Virginia Russell
Magical Lore of Animals, Yvonne Aburrow
Magical Lore of Cats, Marion Davies
Magical Lore of Herbs, Marion Davies
Magick Without Peers, Ariadne Rainbird & David Rankine
Masks of Misrule - Horned God & His Cult in Europe, Nigel Jackson
Medicine For The Coming Age, Lisa Sand MD
Medium Rare - Reminiscences of a Clairvoyant, Muriel Renard
Menopausal Woman on the Run, Jaki da Costa
Mind Massage - 60 Creative Visualisations, Marlene Maundrill
Mirrors of Magic - Evoking the Spirit of the Dewponds, P Heselton
The Moon and You, Teresa Moorey
Moon Mysteries, Jan Brodie
Mysteries of the Runes, Michael Howard
Mystic Life of Animals, Ann Walker
New Celtic Oracle The, Nigel Pennick & Nigel Jackson
Oracle of Geomancy, Nigel Pennick
Pagan Feasts - Seasonal Food for the 8 Festivals, Franklin & Phillips
Patchwork of Magic - Living in a Pagan World, Julia Day
Pathworking - A Practical Book of Guided Meditations, Pete Jennings
Personal Power, Anna Franklin
Pickingill Papers - The Origins of Gardnerian Wicca, Bill Liddell
Pillars of Tubal Cain, Nigel Jackson
Places of Pilgrimage and Healing, Adrian Cooper
Planet Earth - The Universe's Experiment, Chris Thomas
Practical Divining, Richard Foord
Practical Meditation, Steve Hounsome
Practical Spirituality, Steve Hounsome
Psychic Self Defence - Real Solutions, Jan Brodie
Real Fairies, David Tame
Reality - How It Works & Why It Mostly Doesn't, Rik Dent
Romany Tapestry, Michael Houghton
Runic Astrology, Nigel Pennick
Sacred Animals, Gordon MacLellan
Sacred Celtic Animals, Marion Davies, Ill. Simon Rouse
Sacred Dorset - On the Path of the Dragon, Peter Knight
Sacred Grove - The Mysteries of the Forest, Yvonne Aburrow
Sacred Geometry, Nigel Pennick
Sacred Nature, Ancient Wisdom & Modern Meanings, A Cooper

112

Sacred Ring - Pagan Origins of British Folk Festivals, M. Howard
Season of Sorcery - On Becoming a Wisewoman, Poppy Palin
Seasonal Magic - Diary of a Village Witch, Paddy Slade
Secret Places of the Goddess, Philip Heselton
Secret Signs & Sigils, Nigel Pennick
The Secrets of East Anglian Magic, Nigel Pennick
A Seeker's Guide To Past Lives, Paul Williamson
Seeking Pagan Gods, Teresa Moorey
Self Enlightenment, Mayan O'Brien
Spirits of the Air, Jaq D Hawkins
Spirits of the Water, Jaq D Hawkins
Spirits of the Fire, Jaq D Hawkins
Spirits of the Aether, Jaq D Hawkins
Spirits of the Earth, Jaq D Hawkins
Stony Gaze, Investigating Celtic Heads John Billingsley
Stumbling Through the Undergrowth , Mark Kirwan-Heyhoe
Subterranean Kingdom, The, revised 2nd ed, Nigel Pennick
Symbols of Ancient Gods, Rhiannon Ryall
Talking to the Earth, Gordon MacLellan
Talking With Nature, Julie Hood
Taming the Wolf - Full Moon Meditations, Steve Hounsome
Teachings of the Wisewomen, Rhiannon Ryall
The Other Kingdoms Speak, Helena Hawley
Transformation of Housework, Ben Bushill
Tree: Essence of Healing, Simon & Sue Lilly
Tree: Essence, Spirit & Teacher, Simon & Sue Lilly
Tree Seer, Simon & Sue Lilly
Through the Veil, Peter Paddon
Torch and the Spear, Patrick Regan
Understanding Chaos Magic, Jaq D Hawkins
Understanding Past Lives, Dilys Gater
Understanding Second Sight, Dilys Gater
Understanding Spirit Guides, Dilys Gater
Understanding Star Children, **NEW** Dilys Gater
The Urban Shaman, Dilys Gater
Vortex - The End of History, Mary Russell
Warp and Weft - In Search of the I-Ching, William de Fancourt
Warriors at the Edge of Time, Jan Fry
Water Witches, Tony Steele
Way of the Magus, Michael Howard
Weaving a Web of Magic, Rhiannon Ryall
West Country Wicca, Rhiannon Ryall
What's Your Poison? vol 1, Tina Tarrant
Wheel of the Year, Teresa Moorey & Jane Brideson
Wildwitch - The Craft of the Natural Psychic, Poppy Palin
Wildwood King , Philip Kane

A Wisewoman's Book of Tea Leaf Reading, Pat Barki
The Witch's Kitchen, Val Thomas
Witches of Oz, Matthew & Julia Philips
Wondrous Land - The Faery Faith of Ireland by Dr Kay Mullin
Working With Crystals, Shirley o'Donoghue
Working With Natural Energy, Shirley o'Donoghue
Working With the Merlin, Geoff Hughes
Your Talking Pet, Ann Walker

FREE detailed catalogue and FREE 'Inspiration' magazine

Contact: Capall Bann Publishing, Auton Farm, Milverton, Somerset, TA4 1NE